S0-BPI-997

A WORLD BANK COUNTRY STUDY

Regaining Fiscal Sustainability and Enhancing Effectiveness in Croatia

A Public Expenditure and Institutional Review

HJ
1869.5
.R34
2002
West

The World Bank
Washington, D.C.

Copyright © 2002
The International Bank for Reconstruction
and Development/THE WORLD BANK
1818 H Street, N.W.
Washington, D.C. 20433, U.S.A.

All rights reserved
Manufactured in the United States of America
First printing March, 2002
1 2 3 4 05 04 03 02

World Bank Country Studies are among the many reports originally prepared for internal use as part of the continuing analysis by the Bank of the economic and related conditions of its developing member countries and of its dialogues with the governments. Some of the reports are published in this series with the least possible delay for the use of governments and the academic, business and financial, and development communities. The typescript of this paper therefore has not been prepared in accordance with the procedures appropriate to formal printed texts, and the World Bank accepts no responsibility for errors. Some sources cited in this paper may be informal documents that are not readily available.

The findings, interpretations, and conclusions expressed in this paper are entirely those of the author(s) and should not be attributed in any manner to the World Bank, to its affiliated organizations, or to members of its Board of Executive Directors or the countries they represent. The World Bank does not guarantee the accuracy of the data included in this publication and accepts no responsibility for any consequence of their use. The boundaries, colors, denominations, and other information shown on any map in this volume do not imply on the part of the World Bank Group any judgment on the legal status of any territory or the endorsement or acceptance of such boundaries.

The material in this publication is copyrighted. The World Bank encourages dissemination of its work and will normally grant permission promptly.

Permission to photocopy items for internal or personal use, for the internal or personal use of specific clients, or for educational classroom use, is granted by the World Bank provided that the appropriate fee is paid directly to Copyright Clearance Center, Inc., 222 Rosewood Drive, Danvers, MA 01923, U.S.A., telephone 978-750-8400, fax 978-750-4470. Please contact Copyright Clearance Center prior to photocopying items.

For permission to reprint individual articles or chapters, please fax your request with complete information to the Republication Department, Copyright Clearance Center, fax 978-750-4470.

All other queries on rights and licenses should be addressed to the World Bank at the address above, or fax no. 202-522-2422.

ISBN: 0-8213-5107-9
ISSN: 0253-2123

Library of Congress Cataloging-in-Publication Data has been applied for.

CONTENTS

Tables

Figures

Boxes

Tables in Annex A

Tables in Annex D

ABSTRACT

The Government of Croatia inherited an extremely delicate fiscal situation when it took office in January 2000. Extraordinarily high public sector spending that surpassed already high tax revenues, combined into record high fiscal deficits. Furthermore, the fiscal situation was undermining the stabilization effort, necessitating a tight monetary policy stance, which contributed to high interest rates and put further pressures on an already delicate banking sector and on the exchange rate. The new Government acknowledged the fragility of the fiscal situation and together with fighting unemployment, made regaining fiscal sustainability a key policy priority. But the situation was complicated by the fact that a high share of public resources were allocated to social spending and public sector salaries within a context of high unemployment. Defense spending, while still high, had already been substantially reduced; while revenue collection expansion, if feasible, would have not been desirable on competitiveness grounds.

Recognizing these circumstances, this Report provides a medium-term analysis of fiscal sustainability, quantifies the size of the necessary adjustment, and identifies and analyzes key areas for expenditure reorientation and restructuring. The overall objective of the Report is to help the Government achieve a durable and sustainable reduction in overall public sector expenditures, while enhancing the effectiveness of public spending. The Report finds that policy measures to support a necessary expenditure reduction ought to be aimed at reducing the public sector wage bill, rationalizing the system of social transfers, and further reducing the size of the defense sector. The reduction of the public sector wage bill is to be achieved through a combination of wage moderation policies and a reduction in the public sector workforce. A redesign of the government structure of wages is also needed to restore horizontal fairness across ministries. Furthermore, social transfers are to be revised and changes imposed to improve coordination among different programs with the aim of reducing differential benefits between privileged groups and the rest of the population and improve targeting. The Report finds that one crucial element of public sector reform in Croatia is a reorganization of budgetary management practices. Reforms in institutional arrangements and processes would allow policy makers to take strategic policy decisions based on informed analysis of public expenditure issues, would allow proper monitoring and auditing of expenditures and would make budgetary choices and outcomes transparent to all elements of society. Consequently the Report provides a detailed list of policy recommendations in this area, which includes: the inclusion of all Extra Budgetary funds into the budget; the inclusion of all source of public sector revenues into the budget; and the adoption of committed-based accounting to resolve the over-commitment of funds.

ACKNOWLEDGMENTS

This Public Expenditure and Institutional Review (PEIR) is based on the findings of a mission that visited Croatia in September 2000, and later consultations and discussions held with Croatian officials over the course of its preparation. The PEIR also benefited of substantial sectoral expertise accumulated through different Bank lending activities in Croatia. The report analyzes expenditures and institutional developments in the public sector proposing a reform agenda aimed at regaining sustainability by reducing public spending while increasing its effectiveness. The task was carried out in close collaboration with the MoF which established a counterpart steering group (headed by the Deputy Minister of Finance) and a technical working group to facilitate consultations in the preparation of this report. In addition, the task benefited from the interaction with various other ministries and agencies, as well as with research institutes and NGOs. The work was also strongly supported by USAID and other bilateral donors.

The team was led by Marcelo Bisogno (ECSPE, team leader) and Sanja Madzarevic-Sujster (ECSPE), under the supervision of Kyle Peters (ECSPE, Sector Manager Macroeconomics 2). Team members and their tasks were as follows: Sue Ellen Berryman (consultant, education sector), Marcelo Bisogno (ECSPE, public sector spending and contributions to education), Craig Burnside (DECRG, macroeconomics and fiscal sustainability), Paulette Castel (ECSPE, pension), Mukesh Chawla (ECSHD, health sector), Ilker Domac (ECSPE, macroeconomics and fiscal sustainability), William Dorotinsky (PRMPS and formerly US Treasury advisor with USAID, budget management), Ivan Drabek (consultant, education sector), David Lindeman (ECSHD, pension), Philip O'Keefe (ECSHD, social protection and contributions to pension), Peter Parker (ECSIN, transport), Sanja Madzarevic-Sujster (ECSPE, public sector spending plus contributions to health and education), Philip Thomas (consultant, public sector employment). Contributions to this report were also made by Zoran Anusic (ECSHD, pension), Elena Katlerova (ECSIN, transport) and Joe Colombano (ECSHD, education). Besides the production of the individual sectoral reports, additional tasks were carried out by Philip O'Keefe (coordination of social sector team) and Ivan Drabek (compilation of health, education, and civil service information). The final report benefited enormously from the supervision and continuous advice from Kyle Peters, who was directly involved in the final stages of its production.

The team benefited from the close collaboration with government officials; in particular, with Deputy Minister of Finance Mr. Damir Kustrak and his team at the Macroeconomic Department led by Ms. Ivana Plese. Mission members had the opportunity to discuss the main findings of the report with different officials from the MoF, Ministry of Labor and Social Affairs, Ministry of Health, Ministry of Education, Ministry of Transport, Ministry of Defense, Ministry of Justice, Croatian Health Insurance Institute and sub-national government officials in Zagreb and Kutina. The report gained also from the views of researchers at the Institute of Economics and the Institute of Public Finance in Zagreb.

The PEIR gained from valuable comments, suggestions and guidance received at different stages of production from: Andrew Vorkink (ECC05, country director), Julius Varallyay (ECC05), Sandor Sipos (Croatia, Country Manager), Nicholas Manning (PRMPS), Allister Moon, Gary Reid, Deborah Wetzel (ECSPE); David Shand (OPCFM, peer reviewer) and

Eduardo Somensatto (LCCGT, peer reviewer). This report also benefited from valuable comments and discussion with Hans Flickenschild, Leo Bonato and Riccardo Maggi (IMF); John Crihfield (USAID) and Jean Tesche and Laura Trimble (U.S. Department of Treasury). A QAG team composed of: Ben Varon, David Yuravlivker and Young Kimaro, reviewed this Report and contributed with their valuable comments to its enhancement.

The authors will like to express their sincere gratitude to the various ministries, agencies and local authorities in Croatia for the time they spent with the team in open and friendly discussions. Their cooperation made this report possible. In particular, special thanks are due to the Minister and Deputy Minister of Finance. Many thanks also to Sandor Sipos (ECCHR, Country Manager, Croatia) and the staff of the Country Office in Zagreb, for their hospitality and support to mission members during the preparation of this report and to our colleagues at the IMF and USAID for close collaboration. Finally, special thanks to Kathryn Rivera (ECSPE) for her outstanding work and patience in processing this report; and to Anita Correa who was responsible for processing this final version of the report.

ABBREVIATIONS AND ACRONYMS

BED	Budget Execution Department	LFS	Labor Force Survey
BRA	Bank Rehabilitation Agency	LGs	Local Governments
BSO	Budget Supervision Office	MMATC	Ministry of Maritime Affairs, Transport and Communications
CCG	Consolidated Central Government	MoE	Ministry of Economy
CEE	Central and Eastern Europe	MoF	Ministry of Finance
CEECs	Central and Eastern European Countries	MOES	Ministry of Education and Sports
CEFTA	Central European Free Trade Agreement	MST	Ministry of Science and Technology
CG	Central Government	MTEF	Medium Term Expenditure Framework
CGG	Consolidated General Government	NATO	North Atlantic Treaty Organization
CHII	Croatian Health Insurance Institute	NGOs	Nongovernmental Organizations
CIT	Corporate Income Tax	OECD	Organisation for Economic Co-operation and Development
CNB	Croatia National Bank	O&M	Operation and Maintenance
CPI	Consumer Price Index	PAYG	Pay-As-You-Go
CPF	Croatian Privatization Fund	PSOs	Public Service Obligations
CBS	Central Bureau of Statistics	PBZ	Privredna Banka Zagreb
DEM	German Mark	PEIR	Public Expenditure and Institutional Review
DRG	Diagnostic Related Group		
EBF	Extra-Budgetary Fund	PF	Pension Fund
EU	European Union	PIT	Personal Income Tax
FDI	Foreign Direct Investment	SAO	State Audit Office
GDP	Gross Domestic Product	REGOS	Central Registry of Affiliates
GFS	Government Finance Statistics	TYBF	Three-year Budget Framework
GNP	Gross National Product	USAID	United States Agency for International Development
GPs	General Practitioners		
HBS	Household Budget Survey	VAT	Value Added Tax
HBOR	Croatian Bank for Reconstruction and Development	VET	Vocational Education Training
		WB	World Bank
HZ	Croatian Railways	WTO	World Trade Organization
IFIs	International Financial Institutions	ZAP	Institute for Payments
IMF	International Monetary Fund		

EXECUTIVE SUMMARY

The Government faces an unparalleled opportunity to place Croatia on a sustainable growth path, achieve better living standards for all Croatians, and integrate into the European Union. There is also an opening to global markets through Croatia's entry into the WTO. To seize this opportunity, Croatia needs to sustain macroeconomic stabilization and create a better climate for investment. One key challenge in this respect, is public sector reform oriented to both diminish the size of the state, and to reduce the fiscal deficit to sustain macroeconomic stability in the medium term. The Government has already made a good start in this process by reducing expenditures by some 5 percent of GDP and lowering the fiscal deficit. However, as the Government recognizes, substantial further progress is needed. The scope for reducing the deficit through revenue increases is limited, even though a decrease in the tax burden would be highly desirable. This means that most of the adjustment will need to be made in public expenditures, in particular by identifying and implementing policies that will reduce the level of expenditures, while improving their effectiveness. Improving the effectiveness of budgetary management will be critical to the success of this effort. This Report is intended to assist the Government in taking on this challenge.

Croatia has already overcome tremendous challenges during the 1990s. First and foremost, it has undergone the process of nation building. The country, in general, and its public finances, in particular, are still bearing the cost of the effects of the war, both in terms of investment for reconstruction and the cost of mitigating its social consequences. In addition to the war, Croatia has overcome hyperinflation thanks to a successful stabilization program and now enjoys price and exchange rate stability. Yet, the economy has managed to recover growth after a steep collapse in output, the combination itself of transitional recession and war devastation. In doing this, the country took steps in addressing the structural reform agenda. By now, nearly two thirds of the economy is in private hands; more than three quarters of banking assets are in private institutions and the past legacy of close linkages between enterprises and banks has been broken. While the remaining agenda in private sector development and privatization is still large, significant progress has been made in these areas.

Important steps have also been taken in the public sector. As part of the stabilization program, fiscal deficits were kept low. Dramatic increases in expenditures were, until the late-1990s, matched by increases in revenues. Nevertheless, the challenge of nation building, the impact of war, and the subsequent needs for reconstruction, refugees and displaced persons, and to improve the social well-being of the Croatian population, all placed severe upward pressure on expenditures. As a consequence, public sector spending increased by more than 16 percentage points between 1991 and 1999. While the Government reduced expenditures by some 5 percent of GDP since taking office in January 2000, Croatia still has one of the largest public sectors in the region. With tax revenues as a share of GDP at over 41 percent of GDP, Croatia is one of the highest taxed economies in the region. The enormous tax burden borne by the private sector is likely to have driven a substantial part of economic activity underground and reduced profitability in the formal sector.

Beginning in late-1998, fiscal deficits began to rise as revenues ceased expanding and expenditures continued to rise. The deficit of the Consolidated Central Government (CCG) peaked in 1999, reaching roughly 8 percent of GDP on an accrual basis, to be significantly reduced in 2000, to about 5.6 percent of GDP. Up until now, financing of these large deficits has been facilitated by relatively easy access to international capital markets, and by significant privatization receipts. Not surprisingly, the share of public and publicly guaranteed debt to GDP has expanded from 30.4 to 54.2 percent of GDP. The growth of public debt also reflects the bailouts and further recapitalization of several banks and the coverage of the under-funded obligations of the deposit insurance scheme. Rising public debt ratios and deficits are likely to make access to external financing more costly and less abundant in the future. Furthermore, privatization receipts are not a viable long-term strategy as they are expected to diminish significantly after 2003. Moreover, the reliance on privatization receipts may also have an adverse effect on the quality of the privatization process.

The level of public sector spending and the ensuing fiscal deficits are not sustainable in the long run. The results of a fiscal sustainability exercise conducted for this Report indicate that, in order to keep the stock of debt stable as a fraction of the GDP, the Government of Croatia needs to run a primary deficit of no more than 0.3 percent of GDP, which is far below those achieved over the last two years. Moreover, Croatia's public sector is extremely large on a comparative basis. Croatia public sector has also expanded significantly while virtually all Central European economies have reduced the size of their public sectors during the 1990s. As a consequence, private sector-led growth in Croatia has been hampered by a large and expanding public sector that extracts too much from the economy and fails to allocate an adequate share of these resources in support of growth.

The scope for reducing the deficit through revenue increases is limited, as tax compliance is comparatively high in Croatia.[1] Moreover, given the current levels of taxation and unemployment, a decrease in the tax burden would be highly desirable over the medium term. The brunt of the adjustment, therefore will need to be made in public expenditures, in particular by identifying and implementing policies that will reduce the level of expenditures while improving their effectiveness. A critical part of the process will be to improve the effectiveness of budgetary management. Furthermore, the quality of the fiscal adjustment is crucial to its success. The credibility of a fiscal adjustment is enhanced when the fiscal adjustments rely on expenditure reductions. In particular, reductions in transfers and the government wage bill tend to be more permanent and even expansionary. Only after durable and sustainable reductions have been made in expenditures should the Government embark upon tax reform aimed at lowering the tax burden.

Fiscal adjustment is the cornerstone of the Government's strategy. The Government recognizes that the current tax burden is high, and has made it clear that the fiscal adjustment will need to rely mainly on sustainable expenditure cuts. The Government has already taken steps to change the mix of macroeconomic policies, as the policies of the past few years—high fiscal deficits, high levels of taxation and an expansive public sector—have put pressures on macroeconomic imbalances (the current account deficit, inflation and unemployment) and stifled

---

[1] The exception being: payroll contributions; where the introduction of the unified system of collection is expected to improve resource mobilization.

private sector activity. The Government has also designed a medium-term reform program (2001-03) aimed at re-balancing monetary and fiscal policy and revitalizing structural reforms with exchange rate stability. It took a good first step in 2000 but it needs to consolidate and sustain these measures in the medium term through the implementation of its medium-term fiscal program. This program aims to reduce the deficit of the CCG from 5.6 percent of GDP in 2000 to 1.3 of GDP by the end of 2003 which would suffice to place fiscal policy on a sustainable course. Achieving these targets would require broader and deeper reforms, particularly in the civil service and the extra-budgetary funds (EBFs), as the reductions achieved in 2000 through wage restraint and containment in public investment, particularly the latter, are not of the type that can be sustained.

Since the beginning of 2001 – when this Report was being finalized and discussed-, the Government of Croatia started to implement a second wave of fiscal adjustments with the aim of further cutting the CCG deficit by an additional 0.4 percent of GDP. This seemingly small reduction in the overall CCG deficit, nevertheless, would require public spending reductions, in 2001, equivalent to about 4 percentage points of GDP: about 2.4 percent of GDP is needed to compensate for tax reductions introduced throughout 2000 and early 2001; and an additional 1.2 percent of GDP is due to court-mandated special pension payments.

The Government's new policy measures to support the expenditure reduction –the great majority of which are in line with the recommendations made throughout this report- are aimed at reducing expenditures by mainly lowering the public sector wage bill rationalizing the system of social transfers and some revenue enhancement. The reduction of the CCG wage bill by some 9 percent in nominal terms was a key policy measure. This was to be achieved through a combination of a freeze in the basic wage and a redesign of the system of job grade coefficients which to help restore horizontal fairness across ministries, and a reduction in the public sector workforce of about 10,000 employees. Social transfers were to be revised and changes imposed to improve coordination among different programs. This was to involve reducing differential benefits between privileged groups and the rest of the population and, in general, moderating spending on special pensions, disability and home care allowances, maternity leave and sick pay, while improving targeting. Finally, a few revenue enhancement measures included the expansion of co-payments in health and the elimination of the income tax exemption for war veterans.

Many of these measures have now been implemented or are being implemented, such as the reduction in the wage bill, albeit with some delays and more limited than originally envisioned; while others are in the process of parliamentary discussion, such as the reform of the system of social transfers. The delays in implementing the aforementioned changes in public sector wage and the slow pace in implementing personnel retrenchment has narrowed the potential budgetary savings arising from these measures during 2001. Furthermore, additional spending reduction measures will be necessary to achieve the CCG deficit of 5.3 percent of GDP established within the IMF Standby program to compensate for child benefits spending over and above budgeted figures, for delays in health sector reforms and to make room for additional recapitalization of a state-owned bank. These developments, coupled with the worsening external environment, make more compelling the need for a further rationalization of the public sector in Croatia even in the short run. The main objective of this Report is to help the Government meet these challenges, and to implement its own fiscal medium-term reform program. The Report, after an introductory discussion of strategic issues is divided into two parts. First, it examines the composition of expenditures and analyzes key sectoral issues. Second, several developments including, the emergence of arrears, the lack of control on contingent liabilities and the need for strategic choices in the expenditure rationalization effort all point to the importance of reforming Government's budgetary management policies.

ISSUES IN EXPENDITURE ALLOCATION

Any substantial reform of the public sector in Croatia will have to deal with a broad range of issues. This Report has focused on several sectors that have significant equity and efficiency issues and have the greatest potential for generating fiscal savings in the medium term. As a result, the comprehensive examination of the allocation of public expenditures undertaken for this Report identifies the following issues that warrant deeper examination:

- the level of wages and salaries and social sector expenditures, predominantly health and pension, are identified as key factors behind both the high level of expenditures and the latest expansion of expenditures in the public sector;

- wages and salaries are analyzed in depth, as expenditures on this item are far out of level with comparator countries;

- the main sectoral areas of analysis in this Report are pensions, health, education, social assistance and child allowances, transport and defense.

Spending on pensions, health, education, social assistance and child allowances, alone account for more than one quarter of GDP and constitute the largest component of the Budget. Expenditure levels on these sectors are large when compared with other countries; they are also a primary source of the emerging fiscal deficits. There are also major efficiency issues surrounding these sectors. Furthermore, from an equity perspective, while these expenditures are critical to poverty reduction, social expenditures have not been particularly effective in reaching the poor (see box). Similarly defense and police expenditures have been declining, but still remain large (at around 12 percent of total expenditures); while transport expenditures are also large in the Budget and a portion involves subsidies of a number of transport activities and guarantees for large transport projects. Each of these categories of expenditures is examined in detail in the Report and the issues are summarized below. The Report also outlines recommendations that can be taken in the *near term* and those that are of a *longer term* nature. It is important to note that the analysis contained in this Report is only illustrative of the type of analysis that needs to be undertaken throughout the budget to achieve a comprehensive reform of the public finances.

> **Box: Social Spending and Poverty**
>
> Public sector social spending in Croatia is high, reaching 26 percent of GDP (2000) when administrative costs have been subtracted and 35 percent of GDP once salaries of those who administer these programs are included. However, despite the high levels of social spending, their impact on poverty alleviation is relatively low because: social spending is heavily biased towards programs that do not specifically ameliorate the conditions of the poorest, such as health and pensions, and social transfers that are specifically targeted to the neediest have a much lower share in overall spending; and, the relative allocation of funds among targeted cash-transfer programs does not contribute to reduce poverty as the better targeted programs such as Social Assistance receive significantly fewer resources than less well-targeted programs such as Child Allowance.
>
> Source: World Bank (2001).

The Public Sector Wage Bill

Croatia's public sector spending on wages and salaries, at 12.4 percent of GDP, is excessive. The average for transition countries is about 6 percent of GDP. High public sector wages are not due to unusually large employment levels. Croatia's public employment share in total employment is not particularly high when compared with countries of similar income per capita, nor is the share of public sector employment to total population large compared to other CEE countries. This Report finds that public sector salaries are high relative to salaries in the manufacturing sector when compared with other regional economies, even after controlling for differences in education.

One important factor behind the level of public sector wages is the sharp wage increases awarded to public sector employees during 1997–99. In fact, public sector real wages increased by an average 15 percent per year during this period. While the new Government's more restrictive wage policy in 2000 and 2001 has contributed to contain public sector wages; wage levels in the public sector still remain high. Reducing the public sector wage bill relative to GDP and aligning it with that in other transition countries would be a key component of fiscal adjustment. Wage moderation at the level of the CCG would contribute to restrain salary increases in public enterprise as well as in the private sector. In addition, while employment levels are not excessively large in Croatia's public sector, over-employment does exist in key areas. As reflected in the Government program supported by the IMF, the Government's plans to achieve a 10 percent nominal reduction in the CCG wage bill this year include both employment reductions and changes in the level and distribution of wages across the budgetary sector. One critical element in achieving this goal is the implementation of its plans to reduce employment levels, particularly in those areas already identified as holders of excess employment (e.g., Defense and Police) and the plans to harmonize wage categories across ministries through a new employment law on government officials.

Giving the size of the wage bill and past rapid increases in wages, it is urgent to secure control over public sector wages. In the *short term* it is necessary to (i) continue the freeze on salary levels in nominal terms throughout 2001; (ii) proceed with the reduction in employment in those areas the Government already identified as having excess employment (for example, Defense and Police); and (iii) speed up preparation of specially crafted active labor market policies for adjusting military laid off personnel to civilian employment; (iv) control wage increases in public enterprises in light of existing links between wages in public enterprises and the CG. In the *longer term*, in addition to the continuation of restrictive income policies, it is recommended to: (i) undertake a comprehensive review of the civil service and assign a separate government unit in charge of the rationalization of public sector employment; (ii) assess the current structure of employment according to the existing needs, identify areas of duplication and design and carry out an employment rationalization plan; (iii) identify services that could be contracted-out without affecting the quality of service provision and that could generate savings for the public sector; (iv) offset increases in local governments' (LGs) employment associated with the ongoing devolution of functions from the CG to LGs, by reductions of CG employment.

Health

Health spending has expanded requiring increasing CG transfers to the Health fund. Overall health expenditures, at more than 9 percent of GDP, are 3.5 percent of GDP above the levels of comparable countries. Moreover, public spending on health is around 7 percent of GDP, almost double European levels. Increasing costs, a decreasing number of health insurance contributors and substantial contribution exemptions have all combined to yield significant deficits and payment arrears.

The measures undertaken so far to contain costs and improve efficiency, such as hard budget caps for hospitals and co-payment for drugs, have produced some positive results. However, these reforms have not eliminated distortions in the existing incentive system that pays hospitals on the basis of the cost of delivered services and encourages the use of specialist services, which induces an over-consumption of health care services and works against cost containment. The short-term measures have failed to address the underlying incentive problem and thus, to prevent the existing *overuse of specialist and hospital care* services that characterize the system. A deeper reform to the health sector will have to address the incentive problem.

The current structure of co-payments raise efficiency issues and limit cost recovery options. The usage of health services has been increasingly dominated by usage of specialist and hospital care and has shifted away from less expensive primary care. Inadequate pricing in the form of a compressed structure of co-payments is one important cause. A less compressed structure for co-payments would help shift the use of health services away from more costly secondary care and towards primary care, improving efficiency in the system, and reducing costs. Moreover, the level of co-payments, which still remain quite low, hinders cost recovery in the system. Furthermore, a broad range of co-payment exemptions further reduces cost recovery options in the health system and contributes to distort incentives. Not surprisingly, co-payments, which in other European countries are a significant source of revenues (in the range of 7-10 percent of total health revenues), represent less than 1 percent of total revenues in Croatia.

Recommendations include, in the *short term*: (i) increasing co-payments further; (ii) decreasing co-payment exemptions by limiting them to children, the unemployed and those receiving targeted social assistance; (iii) introducing reference pricing for *medical supplies;* and (iv) implementing an immediate freeze on nominal wages in the sector. In the *long term* it is recommended to: (i) introduce a prospective type of payment system for hospital care-- Diagnosis-Related Group system (DRGs); (ii) reduce social welfare type expenditures currently financed through the health insurance, such as reimbursement for funeral expenses, traveling expenses and transportation costs; and (iii) reduce transfers from health insurance to households in the form of sick pay, maternity benefits, etc. Finally, the system would benefit from expanding private sector participation in the long run. In fact, the transition to private practice at the level of GPs initiated in 1993 has proven effective and relatively swift. However, there is a broader scope of private sector participation in primary care and in hospital care, particularly for low-intensity services and long-term care.

Pensions

Increasing outlays and deficits of the pension system are placing a severe strain on fiscal sustainability and have raised concerns regarding the system's sustainability. Unfavorable demographic trends, and the war and transitional recession both combined to deteriorate the pension system financial viability in Croatia, turning pensions into a major source of fiscal stress. Since 1990, pension benefits have swollen from 10 to almost 13 percent of GDP and are estimated to reach almost 14 percent of GDP in 2001. Although, pension earmarked payroll taxes, at 19.5 percent on gross earnings, are relatively high by international standards, revenues from contributions barely cover sixty percent of current spending on pensions. The remaining financing gap is covered by the State Budget with CG transfers to the Pension Fund reaching roughly 6 percent of GDP by 2001. The primary cause of expansion in pension expenditures has been the use of pensions as a social cushion for lay offs, and the entry of new categories of disabled and survivors' defenders from the 1991-1995 war. Government efforts to reduce replacement rates through the use of price indexing have been successfully rebuffed by the all-powerful lobby of pensioners.

Significant equity issues also surround the pension system. Despite large pension outlays, the Croatian pension system does not effectively reduce poverty among the elderly. Half of the pensioners in 1998 received monthly benefits below HRK 1000 -the absolute poverty line in that year. The increase in benefits due to the Constitution Court ruling, later on, modified this picture; reducing to 20 percent the share of pensioners with pensions below the absolute poverty line. Yet, at the other extreme, defender's disability pensions are on average 3.5 times higher than civilian benefits, while defender's survivor benefits are 5 time higher.

Croatia has adopted an ambitious pension reform that will eventually transform the current pay-as-you-go system into a financially viable multi-pillar system. The 1998 reform of the contributory system will, in the medium-term, reverse these dramatic trends, but it will also increase the fiscal burden in the short-term. In the medium and long term, savings from increased retirement age and reduced replacement rates in the first pillar will gradually reduce the size of the contributory part of the system, which will regain balance by the year 2020. However, the overall system, including the non-contributory component, will still be in deficit by the year 2020. Furthermore, in the short-term, transition costs, especially related to the second tier, will require additional funding. Therefore, tight control and further reforms to both the contributory and non-contributory system are needed to resolve the current fiscal crisis.

This Report recommends several sets of measures. As a matter of urgency, the system should: (i) avoid any further cut in payroll contribution rates until the system shows clear financial improvement; (ii) tighten control over qualifications for access to general disability benefits; (iii) improve monitoring of eligibility rules for defenders disability pensions; (iv) refrain from using early and/or privileged retirement for public employment retrenchment purposes in general, and in particular, for employees of the Ministries of Defense and Internal Affairs; (v) reduce early retirement options; (vi) eliminate exemptions or waivers on contributions to the Pension (and Health) fund used in the past to rescue financially troubled enterprises; and (vii) accelerate the full establishment of the Central Registry of Affiliates (REGOS) and transferring to it the wage and service recording system currently under the Pension Institute. In the *long run* it is necessary to implement changes and if needed secure legislation to: (i) revise defenders pension benefits system (especially survivors' pensions); (ii) harmonize benefits levels between civilian, military, police and defenders; (iii) improve revenue compliance, particularly among farmers and self-employed; (iv) index farmers and self-employed minimum taxable base to wage growth; (v) eliminate the preferential treatment of pensioners in the personal income tax. Finally, it is essential to avoid any further delays in the creation of the individual accounts,[2] as this could jeopardize the long-term financial improvement of the contributory component as well as create inequities for younger contributors.

Education

There is no evidence that the education sector in Croatia is overspending relative to other regional countries. The most important challenge in education is the modernization of the overall system, and the implementation of the changes to provide the type of skills and knowledge required by the global economy. To accomplish this, Croatia needs to reform the curriculum by focusing on general skills and abilities valued by the market economy and to add more flexibility to the education system to make it more adaptable to the current changing environment. The sector also needs to become more broadly accessible to the poorest segments of the population. Currently, relatively high returns to education combine with high dispersion of education achievements to contribute to a highly inequitable income distribution. This points to the existence of a stratified education system, which fails to operate as a mechanism for social mobility. Access to higher education by the poorest segments of the population is severely limited. At the level of secondary technical or vocational programs (VET), recent reforms (1993-94) were biased against the poor. In fact, this Report finds that by creating three-year VET program options with lower academic requirements that precludes access to a university education, the reform has unintentionally severed the possibilities for poorer students to expand their education. There are no speedy solutions for any of the above mentioned problems; each of them would entail deep reforms in the education system.

The sector would also benefit from changing the input-mix, as there are important issues in the way resources are allocated across and within the different levels of education. It appears that there are issues with the allocation mechanisms (norms), for key non-staff inputs and that allocations across different education levels are also not in line with the Organisation for Economic Cooperation and Development (OECD), as Croatia allocates a higher proportion of its total spending on education to preschool and a lower share to secondary education.

This report also found serious internal efficiency problems in higher education, as only a third of those enrolled complete. In addition, for those who do complete, it takes an average of

---

[2] Planned to take place in January 2002.

seven years to complete the four-year degree programs and five years to complete the two-year programs. There are also efficiency problems in other levels of education, as student/teacher ratios are declining below OECD ratios, especially for secondary education.

In terms of assessing the quality of the output, Croatia lacks any interpretable evidence on the learning of its students. It does not know how they perform relative to Croatia-specific learning standards or relative to students from other countries. Notwithstanding the lack of evidence on their performance, the average Croatian child can expect to complete fewer years of education than OECD counterparts, and mandatory instructional time per year is lower in Croatia than for OECD countries. The number of years of education of teachers is also relatively low, as almost half of pre-tertiary educators do not have a four-year university degree.

The range of the reforms required at each level of education is broad, but the majority of the reforms are of a *longer term* nature. In the *short term,* we would recommend a thorough review of spending allocations within each education level. This should lead to a revision of the budgetary Norms to allow greater flexibility in the allocation of non-wage expenditures. In the *longer-term* there is a need to review input norms for inefficiencies at the preschool level in consultation with local government officials and preschool educators; and eliminate all triple shifts from primary schools. However, even more substantial changes are needed at both Secondary and Tertiary levels. The secondary level needs to (i) increase student/teacher ratios, (ii) eliminate the three-year VET secondary programs, (iii) increase the academic content of four-year VET programs, and (iv) implement policies conducive to increase completion rates. The university level needs to (i) replace faculty-specific entrance examinations with nationally administered and graded examinations, and (ii) implement articles of the proposed Bill on Institutions of Higher Education that target incentives for students to complete programs quickly. In general, Croatia needs to facilitate the expansion of private education provision by clarifying and simplifying the processes and standards that private providers have to meet.

Social Assistance and Child Allowances

Social assistance in Croatia is characterized by poor coordination among the different programs, different eligibility criteria, and programs' rules that are often not clear to beneficiaries and sometimes subject to discretion of local officials. In addition the system also allows for the possibility to collect benefits from multiple sources.[3] This report, therefore, finds that more substantial poverty reduction can be achieved by reallocating funds and improving coordination among existing social programs.

The two most important social programs are the social assistance and child allowances programs. Both these programs are targeted; however, the poverty reduction impact of one HRK allocated to the former is substantially greater than for the latter. Despite these differences, total spending on social assistance was around 0.2 percent of GDP while some 0.77 percent of GDP was allocated to child allowances (1999). Notwithstanding these differences in allocation, the poverty headcount in Croatia would have been around 1.2 percentage points higher without

---

[3] Individuals can benefit from different income census applied by municipalities as oppose to thresholds applied by the centers for social care.

social assistance spending[4] and only 0.8 percentage points higher without child allowances. This suggests a significantly more efficient use of budgetary resources for poverty reduction by reallocating funds towards social assistance. In light of this analysis, recent increases in child allowance spending should by no means be at the expense of social assistance payments, as the latter is better targeted and already has very limited funding.

The *short term* reform agenda with respect to these two programs will involve: (i) a close monitoring of Child allowance spending in 2001, and at the minimum a quarterly review; (ii) adjustments in the eligibility thresholds to the Child allowance if the fiscal pressures of increased coverage become significant; (iii) a reconsideration of the automatic eligibility for child allowances of specific groups such as defenders' families in case where there are no solid evidence of them being categorically poorer than average. In the *medium term*, it will be necessary to: (i) review the coverage and incidence of child allowances, as well as their poverty alleviation relative to social assistance and (ii) reallocate the relative funding of these two programs accordingly.

Transport

Croatia has achieved a great deal in the transport sector in the short time since independence, repairing most war damage, writing laws that are generally suitable to govern the transport sector of a sovereign state, and privatizing some transport enterprises. However, this Report identifies a number of issues in the sector that need to be addressed: the State still dominates the transport sector to an excessive degree; the efficiency of most transport organizations remains low; public sector spending in transport is high; while new investment projects in motorways are prioritized at the expense of maintenance of the relatively abundant existing capacity.

Croatia initiated --under the previous government-- an ambitious program of transport investments much of which appears uneconomic. This is worrisome, as in general, there is ample transport capacity in the country, although much of it remains in fair or poor conditions. This, in turn, is the result of maintenance deferral and the prioritization of major new investments, primarily in motorways. Moreover, the efficiency of most transport operations is low resulting in high transport costs and a poor quality of service.

Croatia aspires to join the European Union (EU) where transport is overwhelmingly market oriented. There is significant scope for privatization and commercialization within the sector, as well as for reorienting the Government's direct management of the transport sector. This will also help to prepare transport enterprises to compete in the EU and reduce total public transport expenditures.

The situation of the sector, therefore, calls for a multi-pronged approach. In the *short to medium term*: (i) prioritize maintenance and rehabilitation of existing transport infrastructure, primarily highways at the expense of new investments; (ii) rank new investments based on cost/benefit assessments deferring those with economic rates of return less than 12 percent until

---

[4] When including all cash assistance allowances including payments outside the support allowance (equivalent to 0.54 percent of GDP in 1999).

traffic develops; (iii) estimate---using actuarial techniques---the cost of guarantees and other contingent liabilities and include them in the 2002 budget. In the *longer term*: (i) minimize the use of guarantees and other extra-budgetary obligations; (ii) provide operating subsidies only where they are justified on social grounds, for example, suburban passenger services or inter-island ferries; and finally (iii) define and implement a coherent strategy to reduce the role of the Government in the transport sector and privatize existing transport operations. If these recommendations are pursued, it should be possible to bring, in the medium term, total unconsolidated public transport expenditures down to 3 percent of GDP (or less than 2 percent of GDP on a consolidated basis) which is closer to the norm for middle income countries.

Defense

Croatia has made considerable progress in reducing and rationalizing defense expenditures. Starting in 1999, a more transparent presentation of the defense budget has facilitated a more thorough discussion of defense issues, inducing the Government to implement a further rationalization of defense spending and introduce better budget management. In aggregate, Croatia's spending on defense stands at 2.9 percent of GDP (2000, accrual basis) down from 9.4 percent of GDP at its peak in 1995.

Despite the progress already achieved in reducing defense outlays, the Government has indicated that is committed to achieve further reductions in the sector bringing outlays more in line with other European countries. Given the current cost structure of the defense sector in Croatia, cutbacks are planned to be heavily concentrated in personnel reductions. In fact, currently, almost 70 percent of spending in defense is allocated to wages and related compensations. This appears to be out of line with defense spending patterns in NATO member countries, where there is much higher spending on equipment. If the Government were to achieve defense levels in line with the average for Western-European countries through cuts in personnel; the savings from a reduced wage in the order of one percent of GDP would be partially offset by social costs related to layoffs estimated to be in the amount to 0.46-0.59 percent of GDP in the first year of adjustment. This cost would fall in the subsequent years to an amount ranging from 0.1 to 0.6 percent of GDP depending on the options chosen. The sector should identify and divest real state property and other non-core assets owned by the Ministry, not required for defense purposes, in order to further reduce related maintenance and administration costs.

ISSUES IN BUDGET MANAGEMENT

The external review of expenditures contained in this Report provides some clear indications of areas where a reorientation and restructuring of expenditures are required. However, the expenditure review does not provide by itself, a complete analysis of expenditure issues in Croatia nor can it substitute for a political process that determines strategic priorities for the government. A crucial element of public sector reform is a reform of its budgetary management practices. This would ensure that institutional arrangements and processes operate in such a way that allow policy makers to make strategic policy choices based on an informed analysis of public expenditure issues. An effective management of the budget would ensure that expenditures are properly monitored and audited. It would also make budgetary choices and outcomes transparent to all elements of society.

Croatia has already made significant progress in improving public expenditure management in the past decade. In fact, Croatia managed to reform the Social Accounting Office in the early 1990's; established an external audit body (the State Audit Office, in 1993); passed a new budget law (1994); introduced a 3-year rolling Public Investment Program (1996); and is in the process of implementing a Single Treasury Account. These developments are all the more impressive when one realizes that they occurred against a backdrop of transitioning to a market economy, establishing an independent nation, enduring an armed conflict and subsequently, restructuring a war-torn economy. However, there is much to do in improving budgetary management. This report identifies several areas where further improvement in the system is necessary.

First, the analysis undertaken in this Report indicates that the current budget in Croatia is not a comprehensive measure of all fiscal activity in four key aspects:

- five extra-budgetary funds are not included in the budget;
- off-budget revenues, outside of the extra-budgetary funds, still exist;
- the cash budgeting system leads to the accumulation of arrears that do not appear in budget presentations;
- laws outside of the budget law lead to mandatory spending that falls outside the budget process.

This Report strongly recommends that all extra-budgetary funds, and off-budget revenues be brought onto the Budget. It also recommends a number of steps for expenditure control and monitoring that would limit the occurrence of arrears.

Second, the Croatian budget formulation process is highly dispersed, with a great deal of responsibility for budget formulation and prioritization placed with line ministries. The Government relies heavily on each line Ministry for assuring that sectoral policies are optimal, spending is efficient and effective, and programs operate under sound financial principles. Currently, the MoF has limited capacity to develop budget options, push public finance reforms, monitor and control spending, and enforce current laws and regulations. In the current set up, there is no analysis of current agency spending or questions to ministries probing the assumptions underlying current spending allocations or even probing the spending agency definition of "needs." As a result, the current public finance system in Croatia presents very limited mechanisms for accountability, whether over finances, policy, or actual spending program results. The MoF should play a more fundamental role in setting standards, coordinating government-wide financial issues, analyzing policy issues and budget developments and supporting central decision-making bodies (for example, Cabinet). The public sector would benefit from a more robust budget process, led by a stronger actor at the center of budget formulation. This would result in more accountability and substantive dialogue; making the budget process an instrument for challenging line agencies to improve performance and holding managers accountable for resource utilization.

Third, the current system of Expenditure Control reduces flexibility to the operation of agencies while absorbs too much administrative resources. Currently, the Budget allocates spending in an extremely disaggregated and detailed manner ("third level" of the chart of accounts; i.e., a "budget position"). Spending is controlled against these positions. This level of disaggregation is counterproductive as a *control* approach. Even worse, it essentially freezes in place the current method of operations of spending units. Agencies need more flexibility to adapt to changing circumstances; the current itemization of spending hinders their search for alternate organization and delivery methods.[5]

Fourth, the current Budget Execution function is divided among several offices, with no office assigned the lead for coordinating the entire process. Under the current system, each ministry submits its financial plans for the year, which is based on the "agreement" reached in budget preparation. These financial plans are modified to reflect the cash position of the Government, and become the basis for budget execution (payments order processing) by the Budget Execution Department. Then, the Budget Execution Department practices cash rationing—limiting the payments to available cash balances. There is no monitoring or control of commitments, which all but guarantees the build-up of arrears. In this regard, this Report recommends the adoption in the short term of modified accrual budgeting and accounting. The full adoption of the single Treasury Account will improve cash management in the medium term. The adoption of a treasury single account, however, will not, by itself, solve the problem of arrears; as most of the current arrears stem from over-commitment of funds and not poor cash management.

Fifth, the current Internal Control and Auditing functions in Croatia rest on the hands of the ministries. Primary responsibility for internal control is placed with each Minister, who is also responsible for internal control and auditing of all spending agencies under his/her Ministry. The MoF has a Budget Supervision Office (BSO) that acts as the government-wide internal auditor and which is supposed to monitor legal usage of budget revenues and expenditures and advise on regulations affecting state expenditure. The BSO inspects accounting and financial documents, with the mission to cover: extra-budgetary funds, local governments, and public enterprises. However, the last two are not being covered due to insufficient staff. Staff restrictions also limit the ability of the BSO to follow-up audits in order to assess whether previously identified irregularities have been corrected and to follow-up with enforcement agencies on the effective application of penalties. Finally, the Budget Execution Department and the Budget Consolidation Department do not use their influence to enforce BSO findings or push for corrections of irregularities. This Report recommends that until internal auditing and control are institutionalized in the government, budget supervision audits should be conducted through to the end user or recipient of funds. It is also recommended that the Budget Law be amended to formally establish the Office within the Ministry of Finance, as an independent department reporting to the Minister or Deputy Minister of Finance.

Sixth, the Croatian Parliament---the Sabor---should develop capacity to participate more actively and be able to play a more fundamental role in the budget process; both in budget formulation and oversight. However, the Sabor is not consulted by the Government or involved in budget formulation until the Budget is formally proposed by the Government. The current budget submission from the Government lacks the necessary information for the Sabor and Budget Committee to ascertain what is happening. The Sabor's role in monitoring the budget

---

[5] Although the budget law allows the transfer of up to 5 percent of a "position" to another "position" within the Ministry, after Ministry of Finance approval, this generates enormous paperwork and information processing burdening agencies and ministries for no apparent benefit.

execution process is largely reactive. If the budget is out of balance during the year, theoretically the Sabor could take direct action, but in practice, it only does what the Government requests. No real enforcement mechanism exists to penalize those responsible for overspending. For the Sabor to play a more active role in the Croatian budget process, the Parliament in general, and its Budget Committee, in particular, need to count with appropriate staff support. Staffing the Sabor with adequate analytical capacity would allow it to engage the Government on substantive policy issues regarding the budget process.

CHAPTER 1: THE STRATEGIC SETTING

INTRODUCTION

The new Government faces an unparalleled opportunity to place Croatia on a sustainable growth path, achieve better living standards for all Croatians, and integrate into the European Union. There is also an opening to global markets through Croatia's entry into the WTO. To seize this opportunity, Croatia needs to sustain macroeconomic stabilization and create a better climate for investment. One key challenge in this respect is public sector reform, both to reduce the size of the state, and to reduce the fiscal deficit to sustain macroeconomic stability in the medium term. The scope for reducing the deficit through revenue increases is limited and indeed a decrease in the tax burden would be highly desirable. This means that most of the adjustment will need to be made in public expenditures, in particular by identifying and implementing policies that will reduce the level of expenditures, while improving their effectiveness. Improving the effectiveness of budgetary management will be critical to the success of this effort.

To this end, the Government has formulated an economic strategy for 2001–04. The centerpiece of the Government's program is fiscal adjustment, wage discipline, and continued exchange rate stability. The Government recognizes that the tax burden is high, and has made it clear that the fiscal adjustment will need to rely mainly on sustainable expenditure cuts. One key message of this report is that the Government must move first on reducing credibly expenditures and only then, consider further reductions in the tax burden.

Given the extent of the expansion in public sector spending over the last years, and the limited possibilities to expand current tax levels, the necessary spending cuts are by no means small. To accomplish this substantial reduction in expenditures and to do it in a sustainable manner, the Government of Croatia needs to implement structural reforms in key areas, including pensions, health, defense, civil service, local governments and budget management. While this Report identifies key actions and priorities in these areas, the Government needs to improve its own knowledge base of the public sector, and develop analytical capacities in both core and line agencies to examine expenditure issues and assist in making strategic choices.

This report investigates expenditure issues and proposes policy measures to help the Government realize its fiscal objectives. The remainder of Chapter 1 assess the evolution of the fiscal stance in the context of overall macroeconomic policies, analyzes the sustainability of fiscal policy in Croatia, and highlights the key elements of a credible fiscal consolidation. It discusses the nature of the fiscal expansion during the past decade and examines the fiscal deficits that materialized in the latter part of the decade. Next, the Chapter looks at the size of the public sector and finds that Croatia has one of the largest public sectors in Central and Eastern Europe. Moreover, it has one of the heaviest tax burdens in Europe. The Chapter argues that long-run fiscal sustainability would require primary fiscal deficits at or below 0.3 percent of GDP. Finally, the Chapter concludes by arguing that a credible and sustainable fiscal adjustment requires substantial expenditure reductions.

Chapter 2 studies in detail the composition of public expenditures and provides an 'external review' of some key elements of the Government's expenditure programs. It examines in depth the level of expenditures on wages and salaries; the social sectors, in particular, the pension, health and education sectors, and the allocation into the social assistance and child allowances programs. Finally, the Chapter reviews the transport and defense sectors. The sectoral discussions outline potential reform programs and highlight expenditure trade-offs in each of these sectors. These sectoral discussions, also importantly, outline the types of analyses that need to be institutionalized within the Government to evaluate the impact and beneficiaries of expenditure programs.

Finally, Chapter 3 discusses Croatia's existing system of fiscal management, the primary institutions involved in budget management, and the existing legal framework for budget processes. The benefits of expenditure analysis as undertaken in Chapter 2, diminish substantially over time, as government expenditure programs change rapidly. Thus, changes in the process of budget planning, implementation and review offer the best opportunity to fundamentally change the orientation of fiscal policy in Croatia. Developing budgetary institutions and capacities that help policy makers make strategic choices, that identify the effectiveness of public expenditure programs and that ensure transparency so that the budget process has feedback from all elements of civil society, is essential to success in expenditure reform.

THE MACROECONOMIC SETTING

In order to contain hyperinflation, the Government of Croatia (GoC) launched in October 1993 one of the most successful stabilization programs in the region. Inflation dropped immediately from about 28 percent per month in 1993 to negative values in the following year and it has remained low ever since (Table 1.1).

Macroeconomic stability coupled with the resumption of peace (1995) contributed to a strong rebound in economic activity. The initial recovery was followed by rising domestic demand, driven by a surge in consumption and investment for reconstruction. Initially, in the period following the end of the war, this surge in domestic demand was financed by repatriation of capitals, primarily from deposits held abroad. The increased funding of the banking system via these deposit repatriations triggered a bank-lending boom. This supply-driven credit boom led to growing external imbalances, as import for reconstruction activities and domestic consumption increased rapidly.[6] This, in the absence of a commensurate increase in exports, produced a large current account deficit, which reached its peak of 11.6 percent of GDP in 1997.

---

[6] The advancement of purchases to avoid the 22 percent VAT, introduced in January 1998, and the decision to eliminate some import tax exemptions after 1997 also contributed to the surge in imports in that year.

Table 1.1: Croatia: Selected Indicators, 1994–2000

INDICATOR	1994	1995	1996	1997	1998	1999	2000
GDP per capita, current USD	3,137	4,029	4,422	4,398	4,805	4,406	4,179
Real GDP, % growth rate	5.9	6.8	5.9	6.8	2.5	-0.4	3.7
Consumer price index, e.o.p., %	-3.0	3.8	3.5	3.8	5.4	4.3	7.5
Consumer price index, p.a., %	97.5	2.0	3.5	3.6	5.7	4.2	6.2
Labor productivity in industry, pa, % change	3.0	6.6	11.3	11.9	8.7	3.9	4.3
Average monthly gross wages, pa, % change	...	34.0	12.3	21.0	12.6	10.2	7.0
Unemployment Rate (LFS), pa	...	...	10.0	9.9	11.4	14.5	16.1
Current account balance, % of GDP	5.9	-7.7	-5.5	-11.6	-7.1	-6.9	-2.1
Expenditures & net lending of CGG, % of GDP	**44.1**	**48.9**	**51.9**	**51.3**	**53.9**	**56.2**	**51.3**
CGG balance (incl. Arrears) (% of GDP)[a]	**1.5**	**-1.4**	**-2.2**	**-3.0**	**-2.5**	**-8.0**	**-5.4**
Total public debt, % of GDP[b]	**22.2**	**19.3**	**30.4**	**33.1**	**38.3**	**47.8**	**54.2**

a: Excludes privatization receipts.
b: Includes publicly guaranteed debt.
... no data available.
Source: Central Bureau of Statistics, Croatian National Bank, Ministry of Finance, Institute for Payments and staff calculations.

While, initially, the current account deficit was financed by non-debt creating capital inflows (mainly the repatriation of deposits), beginning in 1997 these inflows declined significantly. Croatia, then, began to rely heavily on external debt first and, latter on, on privatization revenues, to finance its growing current account deficits. Helped by relatively low initial levels of indebtedness, and by two successful debt reschedule operations with the Paris Club (1995) and the London Club (1996), Croatia received an investment grading in 1997. This opened the door to broader access to foreign financing. As a result, external debt rose from 25 percent in 1994[7] to almost 53 percent of GDP in 2000—a rapid and unsustainable build-up.

In response to the widening current account deficit, the Government began to tighten monetary policy in early 1998,[8] pushing real interest rates higher and depressing economic activity. This coupled with a reversal in access to foreign credit, as a result of the 1998 Russian crisis, contributed to reduce the current account deficit to about 7 percent of GDP in that year.[9] The monetary tightening, the insecurity generated by problems in the banking system and, latter on, the outbreak of the armed conflict in Kosovo, all contributed to the 1999 recession. GDP fell by 0.35 percent in that year. The recession itself contributed to lower imports and helped maintain the current account deficit at 6.9 percent of GDP in 1999. Propelled by private consumption and exports, the economy pulled out of recession in 2000. While consumption expansion benefited from the large wage increase granted in 1999—particularly within the public sector—exports improved, helped by a recovery in Europe and some real exchange depreciation; but mainly, tourism revenues surged as a result of the renewed peace conditions in the region. Foreign exchange inflows from export of services increased by 10.6 percent in real terms. All this reduced the current account deficit to its lowest level in the last seven years.

---

[7] Once the stock of end-1994 external debt to GDP ratio is corrected by the latter recognition of debts within the context of the Paris and London Clubs (1995-1996).

[8] At that time the CNB introduced reserve requirements on bank's foreign liabilities, rising interests rates and allowing certain appreciation of the exchange rate.

[9] The advancement of imports in 1997 due to the imposition of VAT created an "automatic" reduction of imports in 1998. The elimination of some import exemptions in 1998 also contributed to the reduction of imports in that year.

THE FISCAL PICTURE

This section examines the conduct of fiscal policy in Croatia over the past decade. The scope of the public sector in Croatia is described in Box 1.1. First, this section outlines recent fiscal developments and analyzes the underlying causes of the public sector expansion and the emergence of large fiscal deficits. Next, the section looks at the macroeconomic policy mix and undertakes a fiscal sustainability exercise. Finally, it examines the size of the public sector in comparison to other transition economies and the effect of the public sector on private sector activity.

Overview of Fiscal Developments in the 1990s

Fiscal policy played a key role in the Government's early stabilization efforts, as fiscal deficits were kept relatively low, at or below three percent of GDP until the end of the 1990s. Nevertheless, during this period, the country witnessed, in parallel, a dramatic expansion of public sector spending from Independence (1991) to the end of the war (1995), partly due to the need to introduce a new layer of government and to the resources allocated to the war effort. Total Consolidated General Government (CGG) spending grew from 39 percent of GDP (1991) to 49 percent by the end of the war. This expansion was carried out despite a steep reduction of pensions and public sector wages immediately after Independence. This expenditure expansion continued throughout the post-war period, due to reconstruction activities, social spending linked to the war and the Government's inability to resist social demands aimed at rapidly recovering pre-war levels of consumption. As a result, the size of the Government, as measured by the ratio of CGG expenditure to GDP, expanded by more than 16 percentage points between 1991 and 1999. Recent efforts by the new Government reduced significantly expenditures in 2000.

To reconcile its stabilization program with this expenditure expansion, considerable efforts were made on revenue mobilization. In fact, as a result of successive fiscal reforms, the Government succeeded in improving tax administration and at the same time, made substantial progress in aligning its tax system to international standards. A key step in this direction, was the introduction of the VAT, at the beginning of 1998, which generated an increase in tax revenues equivalent to almost 4 percentage points of GDP in that year. In aggregate, tax collection expanded by 11 percentage points of GDP between 1991 and 1998 with tax revenues as a share of GDP reaching more than 46.8 percent of GDP in 1998, turning Croatia into one of the highest taxed economies in the region.

Beginning in late-1998 however, fiscal deficits began to rise. The expansion of revenues ended in late 1998 amid a contraction of the economy. Expenditures, however, continued to expand. As a result, low fiscal deficits turned to large deficits. High fiscal deficits continued in 1999, with the deficit of the Consolidated Central Government (CCG) reaching roughly 8 percent of GDP in 1999 once privatization receipts are properly accounted for as a financing item and payment arrears, which arose quickly during 1998-99, are included in expenditures. The accrual deficit for 2000 was 5.6 percent of GDP.[10] These deficits were financed by privatization receipts and external borrowing and, up until 1999, by resorting to arrears. These sources of financing can not sustain their trends while some may be likely reaching their limits.

---

[10] Based on end-of-2000 arrears in the order of 3.8 percent of GDP.

Box 1.1: The Scope and Organization of the Public Sector in Croatia

The public sector in Croatia is composed of (1) the Central Government, (2) the Extra Budgetary Funds and (3) the Local and Regional Governments. The Central Government (CG) and the Extra Budgetary Funds (EBFs) combine to form the Consolidated Central Government (CCG); which, in turn, consolidated with Local and Regional Governments (LGs) form the Consolidated General Government (CGG).

The CG, also known as Budgetary Central Government or simply the State Budget; is composed of 19 ministries, 17 offices, 8 agencies and directorates and 8 state administration organizations. There are currently five EBFs: Pension, Health, Child, Water Management and Employment. Under the broader definition of the CG, there are also five public institutions and one bank: the Payment Institute, the Croatian Mines Center, the Croatian Privatization Fund, Croatian Roads, Croatian Highways and Croatian Bank for Reconstruction and Development.[1] LGs are composed of 420 municipalities, 122 cities and 21 counties. The City of Zagreb has a special status of both town and county.

Public administration activities are carried out by state administration bodies: ministries, state administration organizations and county offices (including city offices of the city of Zagreb). Ministries and state administration organizations are CG or state administration bodies. State administration activities are regulated by the law. Some of the activities of the state administration may be transferred to bodies of local and regional self-administration and administration units, or other legal persons holding a 'public authority' status (as stipulated by the law). Ministries and state administration organizations may establish regional units on the levels of counties, cities or municipalities for carrying out state administration activities stipulated by the law. In addition, local branches of county and city offices may be established in municipalities for the purpose of carrying out the state administration activities under their jurisdiction.

Public Sector Components

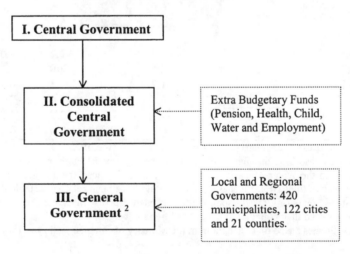

----

1. The Road fund was absorbed into the Central Budget in 1995, being replaced by the Croatian Roads and the Croatian Highways in 2001.
2. The General Government financial reporting excludes the Croatian Privatization Fund (CPF), Bank Rehabilitation Agency (BRA), Payment Institute, Croatian Roads, Croatian Highways and the Croatian Bank for Reconstruction and Development (HBOR).

The latest expansion in expenditures and in deficits has been mainly concentrated in the extra-budgetary funds (EBFs) and in particular, the Pension and the Health Funds. These two funds have combined for a total expansion equivalent to 8.8 percentage points of GDP between 1994 and 1999, of which more than 6.3 percentage points were due to the Pension fund and 2.5

to the Health fund.[11] Revenues from the EBFs declined slightly, as a share of GDP, over the 1994-99 period. This decrease is mainly the result of changes in payroll taxes; as the employer contribution to the Water management fund and the employees' contribution to the Child fund were eliminated in 1998.[12] Without these two changes, the share of EBFs revenues in GDP would have remained at roughly 15.5 percent of GDP.[13] The rise in expenditures of the EBFs and the relative stability of their revenues resulted in significantly increasing deficits.

Table 1.2: Consolidated General Government Finances by Government Level (accrual basis)

| | As a percentage of GDP | | | | | | |
	1994	*1995*	*1996*	*1997*	*1998*	*1999*	*2000*
Total revenue and grants [a]	**45.6**	**47.5**	**49.7**	**48.3**	**51.5**	**48.2**	**45.9**
Budgetary Central Gov.	26.1	27.8	28.5	27.2	30.8	28.2	26.5
Extrabudgetary funds	15.6	15.3	15.5	15.4	15.0	14.6	13.8
o.w. Pension Fund	8.1	8.6	8.7	8.6	7.4	7.4	7.0
o.w. Health Insurance Fund	4.3	4.6	4.8	4.7	5.9	6.0	5.6
Local Government	3.9	4.4	5.7	5.7	5.7	5.4	5.5
Total expenditure and net lending	**44.1**	**48.9**	**51.9**	**51.3**	**53.9**	**56.2**	**51.3**
Budgetary Central Gov.	23.6	26.5	25.6	24.1	25.1	25.7	23.1
Extrabudgetary funds	16.9	18.3	20.6	21.6	23.0	24.8	22.3
o.w. Pension Fund	7.6	9.0	9.7	11.1	11.8	13.9	12.3
o.w. Health Insurance Fund	6.0	7.2	8.6	8.0	8.8	8.5	7.7
Local Government	3.7	4.2	5.7	5.7	5.8	5.8	5.9
Overall deficit/surplus	**1.5**	**-1.4**	**-2.2**	**-3.0**	**-2.4**	**-8.0**	**-5.4**
Budgetary Central Gov.	2.5	1.4	2.9	3.1	5.7	2.6	3.4
Extrabudgetary funds	-1.2	-3.0	-5.1	-6.1	-8.0	-10.2	-8.5
o.w. Pension Fund	0.5	-0.4	-1.0	-2.5	-4.4	-6.5	-5.3
o.w. Health Insurance Fund	-1.7	-2.6	-3.9	-3.3	-2.9	-2.5	-2.1
Local Government	0.2	0.2	0.0	0.0	-0.1	-0.4	-0.4

a: Excludes privatization receipts considered as a financing item below the line.
Caveats: The CG has been absorbing through time the financing of some EBFs. In particular, since 1994, the Road Fund, and since 1998 the Child's and the Water Management fund have been financed from general revenues. Had not been for these changes, the total revenues of the EBFs as a share of GDP would have been relatively stable throughout the 1994-99 period--- at around 15.5 percentage points of GDP. Despite the fall in payroll taxes' rates and the increasing levels of unemployment, this stability has been achieved thanks in part to the upward trend in wages.
Source: World Bank estimates based on cash data from the Ministry of Finance, adjusted for net increases in arrears.

Rising surpluses at the level of the CG have only partially compensated for the increasing deficits of the EBFs resulting in rising deficits at the GG level. In summary, the evolution of

---

[11] Expenses of the Health Fund (CHII) for 1998-99 were also affected by the introduction of VAT for medicines in 1998. In November 1999, the VAT tax rate for drugs was changed to zero and medical disability equipment from the CHII list of coverage became exempted from VAT.
[12] They had been funded up until then from payroll taxes equivalent to 0.8 percent (the Water Management Fund) and 2.2 percent (the Child Fund) of gross wages.
[13] The decrease in the Pension fund's revenues and the increase in the Health fund's relative to GDP, in 1998-99 is in part the result of changes in the tax system. Since mid-1998, payroll tax revenues equivalent to 4 percentage points of gross salaries (2 from employers and 2 from employees) were switched from the Pension and allocated to the Health Fund. In exchange the CHII assumed the cost of providing health services to pensioners, previously paid by a transfer from the Pension Fund.

government finances since 1994 has been characterized by increasing deficits in the GG, the result in turn of growing deficits in the EBFs and to a lesser extent LGs. The deficits of EBFs and LGs have been partially compensated by surpluses at the level of the CG. The overall trend was reversed in 2000, as the new Government reduced expenditures by nearly 5 percentage points of GDP; nevertheless, the EBFs still ran a significant deficit that was only partially offset by a higher surplus in the CG.

Up until now, financing of these large deficits has been facilitated by relatively easy access to international capital markets, and by significant privatization receipts. As a consequence, the share of public sector debt to GDP has expanded from 28.5 to 38.1 percent of GDP from 1996 to 2000; and from 30.4 to 54.2 percent of GDP in the same period once publicly guaranteed debt is added to public debt (Figure 1.1). In addition to the financing of budget deficits, public debt has also grown to finance the bailouts and further recapitalization of several banks and to cover the under-funded obligations of the deposit insurance scheme.[14] Rising public debt ratios and deficits are likely to make access to external financing more costly and less abundant. The use of privatization receipts to finance deficits has also served to release some budgetary pressure, but it is not a viable long-term strategy as privatization receipts are expected to diminish significantly after 2003. This reliance may also have an adverse effect on the quality of the privatization process, as it may induce the Government to adapt the timing and the content of privatization to the financing needs of the budget.

Figure 1.1: Consolidated Central Government Liabilities

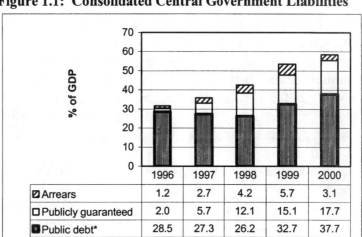

	1996	1997	1998	1999	2000
▨ Arrears	1.2	2.7	4.2	5.7	3.1
☐ Publicly guaranteed	2.0	5.7	12.1	15.1	17.7
▥ Public debt*	28.5	27.3	26.2	32.7	37.7

*It includes the full amount of the London Club debt as public debt.
Source: Ministry of Finance and staff calculations.

Recent fiscal developments have also revealed two other issues that require attention:

(a)   Arrears have emerged as an important fiscal issue, with the Government accumulating unpaid obligations at an estimated rate of 1.5 percent of GDP per year throughout 1996-99 period. Arrears fell for the first time in the year 2000. This accumulation of arrears indicates that substantial improvements in fiscal management are also required (fiscal management is discussed in Chapter 3); and,

(b)   Government guarantees have increased significantly since 1997, when Croatia received its investment-grade rating. Guarantees have been used as a mechanism for the rehabilitation of entire sectors, such as shipbuilding, industry, tourism and agriculture. The limits set within the Budget for the issuance of guarantees were

---

[14] These fiscal activities, however, have not been recorded above the line; therefore underestimating the true size of Croatia's fiscal deficits.

violated in nearly every year. By end-2000, an equivalent 13.6 percent of GDP in financial guarantees and 8.7 percent of GDP in performance guarantees had been issued by the Government. Out of these, an equivalent 16.1 percent of GDP were still active by end-2000. These guarantees represent a significant source of contingent liabilities for the budget and a potential threat for macro-sustainability.

The Role of Fiscal Policy in Macroeconomic Stabilization

From the previous section, we observed that in the latter half of the 1990s fiscal policy was very expansionary. However, assessing the fiscal stance by focusing solely on conventional measures can be misleading as some expenditure and revenue components are sensitive to the business cycle. Thus, a higher fiscal deficit cannot always be attributed to a loosening of the fiscal stance, but may simply reflect that the economy is moving into a cyclical downturn. This problem, to some degree, can be addressed by eliminating the self-correcting cyclical component of the net deficit.[15]

In assessing the Government's fiscal stance, the primary balance is assumed to have two components: the discretionary component or cyclically adjusted balance (which in essence is a policy variable) and the non-discretionary component that moves with the business cycle.[16] The evolution of the actual and cyclically adjusted primary balance, the discretionary component (S^D) is shown in Table 1.3.[17] A glance at Table 1.3 suggests that fiscal policy was contractionary in 1994, 1995, and 1998, while it was expansionary in 1996, 1997, and 1999. The year of 1998 constitutes an interesting example: although there was a primary deficit, the fiscal policy stance was contractionary due to the introduction of the VAT. The fiscal stance, particularly during the expansion/capital inflow period, was not conducive to ensuring stability in at least two respects:[18]

(a)   It amplified economic fluctuations; i.e., it was procyclical, running deficits over two of the highest growth years (1996-97). It forced an increased reliance on external borrowing to finance the deficit after 1995, increasing the economy's indebtedness and making it more vulnerable to changes in the exchange rate and world interest rates;[19] and,

(b)   It was inconsistent with the appropriate policy stance in reaction to a large current account deficit, i.e., a fiscal tightening. As a result of the 'loose' fiscal policy stance, monetary policy was forced to bear the brunt of the policy tightening. Tight money and a loose fiscal stance combined with a wage policy that was inconsistent with the exchange rate commitment. It not only exacerbated the pressure towards

[15] See Brander et. al. (1998) for more on these issues.
[16] For the methodology behind the construction of the cyclically adjusted balance refer to Annex B.
[17] The construction of the cyclically-adjusted budget balance entails the estimation of the output gap—defined as the difference between actual and potential (trend) output—as a business cycle indicator. In the absence of long time series data, we have calculated the level of potential output using a linear trend.
[18] This analysis suggests that fiscal policy was more expansionary between 1995 and 1998 than indicated by the conventional primary balance. In 1994 and 1999, however, it appears that the fiscal policy was more contractionary than what the conventional primary balance would suggest.
[19] It should be noted that such financing also facilitates the maintenance of a more appreciated exchange rate, undermining exports and encouraging imports.

appreciation of the real exchange rate, but also adversely affected the private sector through the resulting high interest rates.[20]

Table 1.3: Evolution of the Components of the Primary Balance (% of GDP)

	Primary Balance (S)	Discretionary component (S^D)	Non-discretionary component (S^N)
1994	2.8	3.7	-0.9
1995	0.1	0.5	-0.4
1996	-1.1	-0.8	-0.3
1997	-1.6	-1.8	0.2
1998	-0.9	0.4	-1.3
1999	-6.3	-2.1	-4.3

Source: Staff calculations.

All in all, fiscal policy during the latter half of the 1990s was not prudent, especially in the context of the macroeconomic setting. The Government's policy mix—higher interest rates and real appreciation—also proved to be harmful for economic activity and financial stability. The alternative—tighter fiscal policy and easier monetary policy—would have been more desirable, not only providing more maneuvering room for the authorities in supporting the banks, but also not exerting upward pressure on interest rates and the exchange rate.

An Analysis of Fiscal Sustainability

Another way to assess the appropriateness of the Government's fiscal stance is to analyze the sustainability of fiscal policy. For the purposes of this report, we have estimated the 'sustainable level' for the primary balance over the medium term[21] required to maintain a financiable level of debt, based on assumptions regarding growth, inflation and the public's willingness to hold money. If we assume under a base scenario levels of inflation (3.5 percent per year) and growth (5 percent per year) the estimated sustainable primary fiscal deficit is 0.3 percent of GDP (Table 1.4). This comes from a combined estimated real debt service cost of 0.3 percent of GDP (this is net of growth's effect on the stock of debt), plus seignorage revenue of just 0.6 percent of GDP.[22]

A number of alternative scenarios were also constructed—based on alternative values for growth, inflation and the real interest rate—to simulate the effect on the sustainable primary surplus (Table 1.4). This analysis shows quite clearly that if growth is more sluggish than targeted (as in the 2 percent growth scenario), then the Government has a choice: run a higher primary surplus (by 1.8 percentage points of GDP), or let debt grow at that rate. The significance of a higher real interest rate is also demonstrated: if agents lose faith that a tight money policy is

---

[20] The effect of the fiscal-monetary policy mix on the exchange rate can be illustrated by a modified version of the Mundell-Fleming model in which it is assumed that the domestic and foreign financial markets are perfectly integrated, thus allowing us to use the interest parity condition as in Dornbusch (1976). In this model, a contractionary monetary policy mixed with an expansionary fiscal policy leads, unambiguously, to an appreciation of the domestic currency.

[21] For details of our analysis see Annex A, which is extracted from the background paper, "*Croatia: Achieving Fiscal Sustainability*" by Burnside and Domac, The World Bank, mimeo, November 2000.

[22] In fact, money demand seems to be so elastic in Croatia that the *maximal* seignorage the Government could raise is not much higher: seignorage is maximized, by a 22 percent inflation rate, at just 1 percent of GDP. This means that even in a high inflation environment the primary fiscal deficit could not be higher than 0.7 percent of GDP.

feasible in the long-run, and the Government starts paying a higher premium on its nominal debt (as in the 11.5 percent real interest rate scenario) the effects on the Government's budget could be dramatic. A primary surplus of 3 percent of GDP might be needed to keep the level of debt stable.[23] Finally, a higher inflation target would do little to help the Government's fiscal position, as the public's willingness to hold HRK is highly elastic with respect to inflationary expectations.

Table 1.4: Estimates of the Short-Run Sustainable Primary Surplus

	Growth Rate of GDP (percent)	Real interest rate (percent)	Inflation Rate (percent)	Sustainable Primary Surplus (percent of GDP)
Baseline	5	5.5	3.5	-0.3
Growth scenarios	2			1.5
	3	5.5	3.5	0.9
	4			0.3
Real interest rate scenarios		7.5		0.8
	5	9.5	3.5	1.9
		11.5		3.0
Inflation rate scenarios			6.5	-0.5
	5	5.5	9.5	-0.6
			12.5	-0.6

Source: Staff calculations.

Based on this analysis, we can conclude that the fiscal policy stance over the last half of the 90s has not been sustainable (Table 1.5), as fiscal policy has moved quite sharply in the wrong direction, at least, until 1999. In fact, except for the year 1998, where the introduction of the VAT moved the adjusted primary balance into surplus, the cyclically-adjusted primary deficit was growing and well beyond the 0.3 percent required for sustainability. This analysis provides strong a priori evidence that fiscal policy in recent years has been moving in the wrong direction. Nevertheless, the year 2000 represents a reversal of the trend seen in the last couple of years, which is a change in the right directions. However, this change is not yet sufficient to bring back fiscal policy onto a sustainable path.[24]

Table 1.5: General Government Budgets, 1997–2000 (% of GDP)

	1997	1998	1999	2000
Estimated Accrual Surplus [a]	-3.0	-2.5	-8.0	-5.4
+ *Interest*	1.5	1.5	1.7	1.8
Implied Primary Surplus	-1.5	-1.0	-6.3	-3.6
+ *Cyclical Adjustment*	*-0.2*	*1.3*	*4.3*	*N/A*
Adjusted Primary Surplus	-1.8	0.3	-2.1	N/A

a: Net of privatization receipts.
Source: Staff calculations.

---

[23] This calculation illustrates a generic fact about sustainability calculations. The initial debt stock and its associated servicing cost have little impact on the calculated sustainable surplus when the real interest rate is close to the real growth rate of the economy. Once the real interest rate exceeds the real growth rate, debt can accumulate very rapidly, and the size of the debt stock becomes important.

[24] Also, the true magnitude of the change in the year 2000 is still difficult to assess, as information on public sector arrears is not yet available.

The Size of the Public Sector

The previous section discussed the sustainability of the fiscal stance concluding that a substantial reduction in deficit levels was necessary. In parallel, this Report has also assessed that the reduction of deficits ought to be achieved primarily through expenditure reduction; notwithstanding the possibility to improve compliance in payroll taxes and further study the possibility of improving non-tax revenues, which seem low when compared to other regional countries. This section looks into the size that the public sector ought to achieve after factoring in all the above changes. In general, there is no 'ideal' size for the public sector and to some extent, the size of a country's public sector reflects voter's preferences in a democratic society. Nevertheless, the above considerations regarding sustainability combined with a target for revenues result in a "sustainable" ratio of CGG expenditure to GDP that Croatia needs to achieve.

Consider a scenario that envisions a slight easing of taxes, so that tax revenue declines marginally to about 40 percent of GDP in the near future. In that case, the analysis above suggests a target envelope for primary expenditure of about 40.3 but certainly no more than 41 percent of GDP. At current interest payment levels, this would result in an overall CGG level of expenditure of around 42-43 percent of GDP. It should be noted that there are two caveats to this estimate. First, in the longer run, it would be desirable for the tax burden on the Croatian economy to be further reduced. In order for this to happen a concomitant reduction in spending will need to occur. Second, the estimated envelope of 40.3 percent of GDP is based on revenue of 40 percent of GDP plus a long-run sustainable primary deficit of 0.3 percent of GDP. This estimate of the sustainable primary deficit was itself based on an assumption that the real interest rate minus the real GDP growth rate is only 50 basis points. For every 100 basis points in additional spread, the expenditure envelope shrinks by the percentage of debt to GDP divided by 100. If the gap between the real interest rate and the real growth rate were 2.5 percent or 200 basis points higher than in the baseline calculation, and that initial debt is equal to the baseline measure (54.5 percent of GDP); then the expenditure envelope would shrink by $2*54.5/100 \cong 1.1$ percent of GDP to 39.2 of GDP.

Another way to assess the Government's fiscal policy is to examine the scope and role of the public sector in overall context of the economy. The role of the Government can be analyzed at a sectoral level; this analysis is carried out in the next chapter. In fact, Chapter II discusses the type of Government intervention in key spending sectors, going into efficiency and equity considerations of the Government's interventions, as well as the potential and convenience for the private sector to take over or complement the public sector in each of the sectors analyzed. In discussing the size of the public sector is also interesting to analyze the relative weight of the public sector in Croatia nowadays both with respect to its own past and with respect to other countries. In particularly with respect to countries in a similar level of development and with similar structural problems such as some of the CEECs. By comparing Croatia's public sector weight to GDP with other CEECs a striking fact emerge immediately: Croatia's public sector is larger. The current size is the result of a very rapid expansion throughout the 1990s, an expansion that has not been experienced by any other transition country included in the comparator group (Table 1.6).

As a result, Croatia's CGG expenditures as a share of GDP reached more than 56 percent in 1999. This level puts Croatia's CGG expenditure not only above most CEECs but also above the majority of more developed industrial countries. In fact, CGG expenditures in countries such as Great Britain, Norway, Spain and Portugal have expenditures to GDP ratios in the 40-47 percent range while countries with higher spending ratios such as Austria, Belgium, Finland, Italy and France are in the 50-54 range. Croatia's expansion in government expenditures is not a necessary feature of a transition country; quite the contrary, other CEECs seem to be heading in the opposite direction. A comparison of the evolution of the Consolidated Central Government expenditures in selected CEECs substantiates this point (Table 1.6).

Table 1.6: Consolidated Central Government Expenditure in Selected Countries

(% of GDP)	91-93 [a]	97-98 [a]	Difference
Albania	48.7	32.7	-16.1
Bulgaria	42.5	32.1	-10.4
Croatia	37.7	45.2	7.5
Czech Rep.	36.0	35.1	-0.9
Hungary	51.7	40.9	-10.9
Poland	44.2 [b]	40.2	-4.0
Romania	36.8	30.3	-6.4
Slovenia	46.1	45.7	-0.4

a: Average over available data within the period; except for Poland.
b: Data for 1994 only.
Source: Government Finance Statistics, IMF; World Bank (for Albania and Slovenia).

An alternative approach to estimate the "appropriate" size of the public sector, is based on comparing the level of public expenditures in Croatia with that in other countries. This approach uses a model that quantifies the effect of factors that are found key determinants of public expenditures.[25] The analysis shows that the actual size of the General Government in Croatia is some nine percentage points above the "predicted" size (Figure 1.2). In general, other CEECs, unlike Croatia, have shown actual levels of expenditure not far away from their predicted values. Croatia's gap, on the other hand, is the largest among all CEECs and the second largest among all transition countries included in the analysis.[26] According to the estimated relationship, Croatia's General Government expenditures should be about 44.1 percent of GNP (or some 43.3 percent of GDP[27]).

---

[25] See Barbone, L. and R. Polastri, *Hungary's Public Finances in an International Context,* in Public Finance Reform during the Transition, The World Bank, Washington D.C., 1998. The model includes factors (such as the age structure and growth rate of the population, income levels and the ratio of public debt to GDP) that reflect social demands as well as the government's ability to both pursue its own policy priorities and overcome its financial constraints.

[26] The transition countries included in the regression—besides Croatia—are: Albania, Armenia, Azerbaijan, Belarus, Bulgaria, Czech Rep., Estonia, Georgia, Hungary, Kazakhstan, Kyrgyz Rep., Latvia, Lithuania, FYR Macedonia, Moldova, Mongolia, Poland, Romania, Russia, Slovak Republic, Slovenia, Tajikistan, Turkmenistan, Ukraine and Uzbekistan.

[27] This number is remarkably close to the one found in the base case of the fiscal sustainability analysis.

As noted in the previous section, throughout the 1990s, the Government reformed the tax system, introducing new types of revenue-generating taxes, such as, excises, surtaxes on the income tax, as well as the all-important VAT. At the same time, the Government also made substantial efforts to improve tax administration. All these efforts contributed to keep fiscal deficits low in the face of mounting expenditure pressures. As a consequence, the level of government revenues and taxation are excessively high in Croatia. Both Croatia's revenue-to-GDP ratio and its tax-to-GDP ratios are the highest among CEECs and the Baltics, and are well above EU levels (Table 1.7). Moreover, the information that is available on tax compliance indicates that it is also comparatively high in Croatia.[28] This implies that there is little room for additional revenue gains from improving tax administration, except perhaps in the area of payroll contributions where the introduction of a unified system of collection is expected to improve resource mobilization from payroll contributions in what is one of the weakest points in tax administration in Croatia. Of more concern, there is the real possibility that compliance could falter as has been characteristic of other transition economies, which would put further pressure on the fiscal deficit.

Figure 1.2: Consolidated General Government's Size: Actual versus Predicted

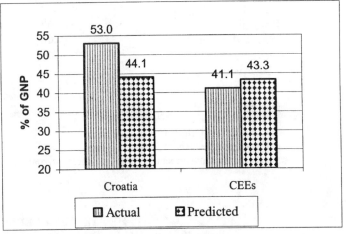

Source: Staff calculations.

In summary, the extremely large size of the public sector in Croatia has had a deleterious effect on private sector activity. The enormous tax burden borne by the private sector has driven a substantial part of economic activity underground and reduced profitability in the formal sector. It is clear that private sector-led growth in Croatia has been hampered by a public sector that extracts too much from the economy while fails to allocate an adequate share of these resources in support of growth.

---

[28] Nevertheless, there is evidence that as in many transition countries, a significant share of formal labor is hired at the minimum wage, possibly indicating that the system of payroll taxes is creating incentives to misreport wage earnings. Moreover, there is also evidence that informal employment is also high, suggesting that payroll taxes may also discourage 'formal' employment.

Table 1.7: Comparative Revenue Ratios (% of GDP)

	Sample Coverage	Total Revenue	Tax Revenue
Croatia [a]	1995-99	50.8	44.5
Central and Eastern Europe			
Bulgaria [b]	1995-98	33.7	26.0
Czech Republic	1995-98	33.9	32.0
Estonia [b]	1995-98	34.2	30.4
Hungary	1995-98	38.6	33.7
Latvia [b]	1995-98	31.3	26.5
Lithuania [a]	1995-97	31.5	30.8
FYR Macedonia [a]	1995-98	39.7	36.8
Poland	1995-98	37.1	33.7
Romania [a]	1995-97	31.0	27.5
Slovak Republic [a]	1995-98	45.9	39.6
Slovenia	1995-98	42.8	40.4
CEE Average [c]		36.3	32.5
EU Average [c]		37.0	33.8
Average of all countries		34.0	31.0

a. Consolidated General Government.
b. Consolidated Central Government.
c. Unweighted average.
Source: IMF; Government Finance Statistics; International Financial Statistics; and IMF staff estimates.

THE MEDIUM-TERM OUTLOOK

This Chapter has reviewed fiscal policy in Croatia over the past decade. From this brief review, it is clear that:

(a)   Croatia's public sector is too large and needs to be reduced to create more space for private sector activity. The size of public sector has expanded while other transition economies have smaller public sectors and have reduced the size of their public sectors in the latter part of the 1990s.

(b)   Fiscal deficits have mounted towards the end of the decade exerting pressure on macroeconomic stability. Up until now, the financing of these deficits has been relatively easy due to the availability of external finance and significant privatization revenues. With a higher debt ratio and privatization revenues likely to decline in the next several years, Croatia needs to lower its fiscal deficits to sustain macroeconomic stability. A tightening of fiscal policy will also allow a better mix of macroeconomic policies, as this will give further room to ease monetary policy, reducing pressures on the banking system and the real sector through lower interest rates.

(c)   The scope for eliminating deficits through increases in revenue is extremely limited. Croatia is already one of the highest-taxed economies in Eastern and Central Europe. Tax compliance is also relatively good in Croatia. Given the existing burden of taxes, a reform based on tax increases would put a substantial new burden on the economy. A lower tax burden would undoubtedly be beneficial to the private sector.

(d)   Moreover, the quality of any fiscal adjustment is crucial to its success. Empirical evidence suggests that the credibility of fiscal adjustment is enhanced when fiscal adjustments rely on expenditure reductions. In particular, reductions in transfers and the government wage bill tend to be more permanent and even expansionary.[29] Only after durable and sustainable reductions have been made in expenditures should the Government embark upon tax reform aimed at lowering the tax burden.

(e)   These factors all point to the need for expenditure reduction to place fiscal policy on a sustainable path. The EBFs, which have been a key underlying cause of the fiscal expansion, will be a critical area to focus the expenditure reduction effort.

(f)   Finally, the emergence of arrears, the lack of control on contingent liabilities and the need for strategic choices in the expenditure rationalization effort all point to the need for reforms in the Government's budgetary management policies.

The Government's Medium-Term Fiscal Plan

The new Government is well aware of the need to reverse the direction of fiscal policy. It recognizes that the mix of macroeconomic policies in the past few years—high fiscal deficits, high levels of taxation and an expansive public sector—have put pressures on macroeconomic imbalances (the current account deficit, inflation and unemployment) and stifled private sector activity. The new Government is embarking on a medium-term reform program designed to re-balance monetary and fiscal policies, moderate wage growth throughout the economy and revitalize its structural reform program. Fiscal adjustment is the cornerstone of the strategy. Fiscal adjustment will be augmented by wage restraint, which will not only reduce the already-high level of public sector wages, but will also reduce wage pressures in the private sector.

Table 1.8: Consolidated Central Government's Medium-Term Program, 2001—03

Percentage of GDP	2000^a	2001^b	2002^b	2003^b
Revenue and Grants	40.5	37.8	36.8	36.3
Expenditure and net lending	46.1	43.1	41.0	37.6
Court mandated pension payments	1.1	2.3	2.2	1.1
Others	45.0	40.8	38.8	36.5
Consolidated central Gov. Balance^c	-5.6	-5.3	-4.2	-1.3
Primary Balance	*-3.9*	*-3.2*	*-2.2*	*0.7*
Memorandum Items				
Inflation (% per year)	6.2	5.0	3.5	3.5
Growth (% per year)	3.7	3.0	3.5	4.0
Second pillar introduction cost	0.0	0.0	1.3	1.3
Change in revenues and grants	-2.3	-2.61	-1.0	-0.4
Change in other expenditures	-5.5	-4.2	-2.0	-2.3

a: Accrual, actual
b: Based on IMF data on Ministry of Finance's three year-framework.
c: Excluding privatization revenues.
Source: IMF and Ministry of Finance.

---

[29] See, for example, Alesina and Perotti 1995.

To guide its reform program, the new Government formulated a three-year fiscal framework for 2001-3 (Table 1.8). This medium-term fiscal program aims to reduce the CCG deficit from about 5.6 percent of GDP in 2000 to 1.3 percent of GDP by the end of 2003. The planned 2003 deficit would imply a primary surplus of 0.4 to 0.5 percent of GDP. Based on the results of the fiscal sustainability exercise prepared for this report, these deficits levels would suffice to bring fiscal policy back to a sustainable course.[30] The Government's medium-term fiscal reform program involves an ambitious program of expenditure reductions that would lead, according to Governments' own plans, to a reduction in CCG expenditures levels equivalent to some 8.5 percentage points of GDP in a period of just three years.[31] The program envisions a significant reduction in wages and salaries, and a rationalization of the health and pension funds. These measures would need to be the cornerstone of any sustainable fiscal adjustment.

The remainder of this report examines how Croatia can implement its program of fundamental fiscal adjustment through a rationalization and restructuring of expenditures and re-engineering of the process of budgetary management, which will enable the Government to better reflect its strategic priorities in the budget. Chapter 2 examines in detail government expenditures and helps to identify areas where expenditure reductions could be made. It is important to note that identifying reforms in the main expenditure programs is not a one-shot exercise, but must be a continuous process of review, analysis and change. Therefore, Chapter 3 analyzes the Government's current budgetary management processes and suggests modifications to the process and the organic budget law that would assist the Government in formulating, implementing and sustaining its own fiscal adjustment program.

---

[30] The planned deficit levels for 2003 would bring fiscal policy back to sustainable levels even if real growth levels fall to around 3.8 percent.
[31] This would lead to CCG expenditure size around 38 percent of GDP and to a GG expenditure size of around 43.5 percent of GDP (assuming LGs expenditures as a share of GDP is kept constant over the period). This would set the size of the government in line with the "predicted" level of expenditures mentioned in Chapter 1.

CHAPTER 2: RESTRUCTURING SPENDING FOR FISCAL RETRENCHMENT

INTRODUCTION

Chapter 1 discussed recent macroeconomic and fiscal developments. It concluded that a significant reduction in the size of the public sector was required to create space for the private sector and to achieve fiscal sustainability over the medium term in light of Croatia's growing debt burden and the likely exhaustion of privatization revenues over the next several years. Since Croatia already bears a very large tax burden, in comparison to other countries in Europe, Chapter 1 concluded that expenditure reduction was needed in the near and medium term to achieve its objectives.

This Chapter examines public spending in Croatia. The Chapter analyzes the expenditures that drove the expansion in the last half of the 1990s. It also investigates the consequences of this expansion at the sectoral level. One key element of the analysis is that it compares Croatian expenditure levels with levels in Western Europe and in the transition economies of Central and Eastern Europe. Even though the analysis in this Chapter is partial, as it does not analyze all sectors, and omits some sectors where expenditure reduction is probably required, it does examine those areas where spending has expanded rapidly and/or is out of line with other transition economies. In these areas, it also attempts to identify where the level of public spending is either excessive, poorly targeted or inappropriate. Finally, in each area analyzed, the Chapter proposes both short and medium-term recommendations for expenditure rationalization.

In this regard, the Chapter illustrates the type of analysis that needs to be undertaken comprehensively in all areas of the budget. It is worth stressing that while there are some important measures identified in the Chapter that can be taken in the short term, the most important measures to contain expenditures in a sustainable way will require a thorough, comprehensive review of the overall expenditure program, not as a one-shot exercise, but as a continuous process of identifying reforms of the main expenditure programs. This will involve choices over time of what the public sector should do, how much it should do, and how it can do it most effectively. Most of these choices are politically sensitive, so an important part of the effort needs to be aimed at developing a political consensus for the need for such reforms. This is why Chapter 3 of this report emphasizes the importance of enhancing budgetary processes, institutions and oversight to help the Government generate its own assessments of program performance and designs. This is needed in order to bring about continuous improvements in the effectiveness of the public sector and the efficiency of public expenditure.

The remainder of this Chapter is organized as follows. Section B analyzes expenditures by economic classification and, in particular, examines spending on wages and salaries, which are excessively large on a comparative basis. Finally, Section C looks at the composition of expenditures based on a functional classification and identifies specific sectors where a more detailed examination of expenditures is required. Specific sectors analyzed include pensions, education, health, social assistance, transport and defense. Finally, Section D looks at the latest developments. The Government began in 2001 to implement a substantial wave of new reforms, most of which are contained in this Report and were discussed with the Government at the time of the Report's dissemination. A brief review of these changes are in the concluding section of this Chapter.

ECONOMIC COMPOSITION OF THE GENERAL GOVERNMENT BUDGET

The analysis of the economic composition of public expenditures in Croatia is based on the Consolidated General Government (CGG) accounts presented in Table 2.1, and on a comparison of the economic composition of the CGG expenditure in Croatia with that in other CEECs (Table 2.2).[32] Several stylized facts emerge clearly from these tables. Not only is the current size of both revenues and expenditures larger in Croatia than in other transition countries, but also some of the components and their latest trends differ substantially from those in other CEECs.

Table 2.1: Economic Composition of Consolidated General Government Operations 1994–2000 (% of GDP)*

	1994	1995	1996	1997	1998	1999	2000
Total revenue and grants	45.6	47.5	49.7	48.3	51.5	48.2	45.9
Total expenditures and net lending	44.1	48.9	51.9	51.3	53.9	56.2	51.3
Current expenditures	40.7	44.1	44.3	44.3	45.6	47.5	45.3
Expenditures for goods and services	25.9	27.8	25.7	23.9	25.5	24.9	23.6
o.w. wages and salaries	10.4	11.9	11.2	11.0	11.9	12.7	12.4
Interest payments	1.3	1.5	1.2	1.5	1.5	1.7	1.8
Subsidies	2.4	2.1	2.2	2.2	2.7	2.8	2.7
Transfers	11.1	12.8	15.2	16.8	15.9	18.3	17.1
Capital expenditures	3.1	4.6	7.2	6.5	7.4	7.6	5.2
Total deficit/surplus	1.5	-1.4	-2.2	-3.0	-2.5	-8.0	-5.4
Primary deficit/surplus	2.8	0.1	-1.0	-1.5	-0.9	-6.4	-3.6
Current deficit/surplus	4.8	3.1	4.6	3.3	5.2	0.1	-0.1

*Accrual basis estimated on the basis of Ministry of Finance cash data, adjusted by net accumulation of arrears.
Source: Ministry of Finance and World Bank estimates.

Comparing Croatia's CGG with that of other CEECs, and the evolution of the composition of expenditure in Croatia, the following facts emerge and are examined in detail in this section:

- Croatia has a higher level of expenditures than the rest of the countries in the comparator group, more than ten percentage points of GDP higher than the average;

---

[32] This analysis is based on estimated accrual basis information; therefore it differs from standard MoF reports on government financial statistics. Accrual estimates were carried out by adjusting officially reported cash data by net accumulation of arrears in the public sector.

- Wages and salaries emerge as the most disproportionate component of expenditures. They absorb almost twice as much in terms of GDP than the average for the rest of the countries, and they have been expanding;

- Transfers, which are mostly channeled to the Health and Pension funds, are at the high end within the comparator group, and they account for a large proportion of the expenditure expansion;

- Subsidies are relatively high. They are concentrated in a few sectors, with a high proportion of them going to the railway company (HZ) and to the agriculture sector;

- Goods and services is the only major budget component that has contracted relative to GDP throughout the 1994-99 period. This is largely due to a large contraction in non-wage goods and services by around 4.4 percentage points of GDP in only six years (1994-2000); larger, in absolute values, than the expansion in wages and salaries over the same period (equivalent to 2.1 percent of GDP). The contraction of non-wage goods and services, however, is highly concentrated in defense.[33]

Table 2.2: Consolidated General Government Revenues and Expenditures in Central and Eastern Europe, 1998 (% GDP)

	Avg.ᵃ	Croatia 1998	Croatia 2000	Albania	Bulgaria	Czech Rep.	Hungary	FYR Macedonia	Romania	Slovak Republic
Total Revenue and Grants	35.8	51.5	45.9	20.3	34.9	41.5	42.9	34.0	34.7	42.4
Current Revenue	35.4	50.8	45.3	20.3	34.6	40.3	41.7	33.9	34.3	42.4
Tax revenue	30.4	46.9	41.4	15.8	27.0	35.6	35.3	31.6	30.7	37.1
Non-tax revenue	4.8	3.9	3.9	4.5	6.9	4.7	6.5	2.4	3.6	5.3
Total Expenditure	39.2	53.9	51.3	30.7	30.5	43	47.3	35.8	38.7	48.3
Current expenditure	34.8	45.6	45.3	25.5	30.5	36.9	41.4	33.8	33.9	41.5
Goods and services	14.8	25.5	23.6	10.2	13.4	19.8	15.1	12	12.6	20.4
Wages and salaries	6.2	11.9	12.4	4.8	2.8	..	7.3	8.6	5.5	7.9
Other G&S	7.8	13.6	11.2	5.4	10.6	..	7.8	3.4	7.1	12.5
Subsidies	1.8	2.7	2.7	0.5	1.8	2.8	2.0	0.1	1.8	3.7
Other current transfers	14.5	15.9	17.1	7.0	13.7	13.2	16.4	21.8	14.4	15.0
Interest	4.4	1.5	1.8	7.8	4.4	1.2	7.8	1.9	5.1	2.4
Capital Expenditure	4.5	7.4	5.2	5.2	1.5	6.0	5.9	1.9	4.0	6.8

a: Unweighted average, excluding Croatia.
Source: World Bank Live Database.

---

[33] Once defense expenditure is excluded, the share of non-wage goods and services in total spending of goods and services remains fairly stable from 1995 to 2000.

Wages and Salaries

Croatia's CGG spending on wages and salaries reached an astonishing 12.7 percent of GDP in 1999. This is almost twice as much as the average for CEE transition economies and even higher than in the majority of the more developed EU economies. In fact, while the average (unweighted) CGG wage bill for transition countries is about 6.2 percentage points of GDP for 1998; Croatia allocated some 11.9 percent of GDP for CGG wages and salaries in that year (Figure 2.1 and Table 2.1). However, despite the disproportionately high level of spending on wages and salaries, Croatia's share of public employment in total employment is not particularly large when compared with countries of similar income per capita. Moreover, the share of public sector employment in the total population is slightly below the median of other CEECs (Figure 2.2).

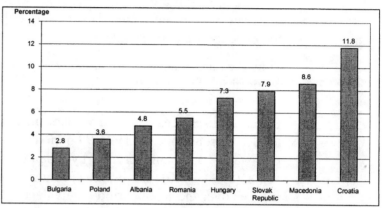

Figure 2.1: Wages and Salaries of the Consolidated General Government (% of GDP, 1998)

Source: Croatia's Ministry of Finance and World Bank.

Croatia's public sector wage bill is at the top of CEECs; but is this the result of high public sector wages or of an overstaffed public sector? At 5.3 percent of population, Croatia's general government civilian employment does not seem excessive relative to a sample of twelve transition countries. Croatia falls below the sample average of 6.2 percent (Figure 2.2). Croatia's ratio of government employment to population is also below the average for 20 OECD countries, for which general civilian government employment averages 7.7 per-cent of population.[34] The high public wage bill in Croatia, therefore, seems to be more the result of high public sector wages relative to other transition economies. Nevertheless, certain areas within the public sector show excessive employment;

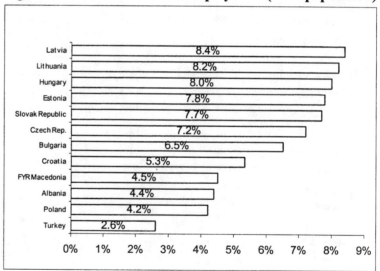

Figure 2.2: General Civilian Employment (% of population)

Source: An International Statistical Survey of Government Employment, World Bank, 1997. For Croatia: Staff estimates based on Central Bureau of Statistics and Ministry of Finance information.

---

[34] Several empirical studies show that affluent countries, in general, have higher shares of public employment than less developed countries.

such is the case of the defense sector in Croatia. Salaries in the public sector seem high relative to salaries in the industrial sector when compared with other regional economies. The ratio of public sector to wages in manufacturing in Croatia ranks at the top of the countries within the comparator group (Figure 2.3). Nevertheless, since the public sector in Croatia employs people with higher average educational attainment than the enterprise sector, it is necessary to control for education differentials to substantiate the preferential wage position of public sector employees.

After controlling for educational attainment, age, experience and other personal characteristics of employees, including the sector of employment, as dependent variables,[35] analysis undertaken for this Report shows that earning premiums of those employed in public administration are second only to those employed in the financial sector. The Health sector, also dominated by public employment, ranked third, immediately after Public Administration and the Financial sector. However, those employed in the Education sector, also almost entirely public, ranked at the lower end of the scale. Wage increases in 1999-2000, which favored public sector wages relative to wages in the enterprise sector, contributed to further enhance earning premiums for public sector employees.[36]

Box 2.1: Public Sector Employment

There are three major employment groups within the non enterprise public sector.

(i)   **"State Officials"**. This group includes Ministers, Deputy and Assistant Ministers and other associated political appointees; as well as judges, magistrates and attorneys in county offices. Their salaries, terms and conditions of employment are set by the Government.

(ii)   **"Civil Servants and Support Staff"**. They are mainly employed in the Central Government and judiciary; with salaries and employment terms of conditions governed by a specific law for the civil service. This law recognizes three major categories of employees: Judicial Officers, Civil servants employed in the state administration (sluzbenici), and Support Staff (namjestenici).

(iii)   **"Public Servants"'** are employed in the service area of the Government (i.e.: education, health and pension). Besides being subject to the Labor Law, they have their own specific law, but in the main, their salaries and additional terms and conditions of employment are negotiated and settled through Collective Bargaining Agreements.

As seen above, the terms "Civil Service" and Public Service" are not interchangeable in Croatia. They refer to different groups of employees within the non-enterprise public sector. Throughout this section, we include the three groups when we refer to public sector employees.

Source: Official Gazette

---

[35] Micro-data from the Labor Force Survey (second half 1998) was used for this purpose.
[36] The analysis is based on 1998 data as the 1999 Labor Force Surveys stop reporting on wages.

Unlike employment in the enterprise sector, public sector employment has not been very responsive to the shift from a state-dominated economy to a market economy. While Croatia's economy has undergone dramatic changes since 1990, there has been a lesser adjustment in public sector employment than in the enterprise sector. The fall in GDP over the 1990-92 period was accompanied by steady and substantial decreases in overall employment levels; this decline in employment reached most sectors of the economy but was mainly concentrated outside the public sector. Employment in the enterprise sector continued declining even after the resumption of growth in 1994 and was the main factor behind productivity improvements. Employment has continued to decrease until now although at a slower pace. Throughout the same

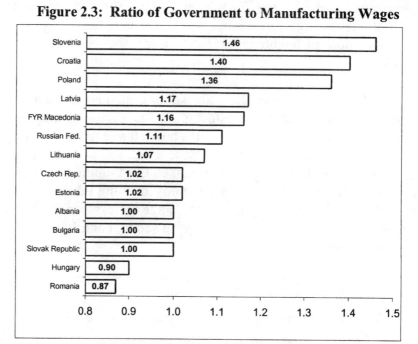

Figure 2.3: Ratio of Government to Manufacturing Wages

Slovenia	1.46
Croatia	1.40
Poland	1.36
Latvia	1.17
FYR Macedonia	1.16
Russian Fed.	1.11
Lithuania	1.07
Czech Rep.	1.02
Estonia	1.02
Albania	1.00
Bulgaria	1.00
Slovak Republic	1.00
Hungary	0.90
Romania	0.87

Source: de Tommaso and Mukherjee, Government Employment and Wages database 2001; for Croatia, own estimates based on CBS information for 2000.

period, employment in the non-economic sphere[37] declined also but much less than elsewhere. Employment in the non-economic sphere dropped by some 12 percent between 1990 and 1992 and it appears to have stabilized thereafter. The large difference in responsiveness of employment in the economic and non-economic sphere raises questions regarding the degree to which the current level and structure of government employment remains appropriate.

While the adjustment in employment was less severe in the public sector than in the enterprise sector, wages in the public sector were subject to steeper reductions in the immediate post-independence period (1991-92). In fact, at the time of Independence, salaries in general, but public sector salaries in particular (along with pensions), suffered a dramatic erosion in their purchasing power due to high inflation. As a result, the share of CCG wage bill to GDP fell dramatically immediately after the start of the war, going from 9 percent of GDP in 1990 to less than 6 percent of a much reduced GDP in 1992. The income policies that emerged from the 1993 stabilization plan also set stricter limits on public sector wages than elsewhere; as a result public sector wages took the majority of the brunt of the adjustment, falling much lower than wages in the enterprise sector.

By 1994, real wages started to grow rapidly over the 1994-95 period. To contain this expansion, the Government attempted to reduce nominal civil service wages by 10 percent in

---

[37] Essentially a proxy for the public sector, this category includes administration, education, health and social welfare.

1995, but was unsuccessful. The following year, the Government decided to impose the principle of zero real wage increases for the following three years (1996-1998). Although unsuccessful again, the failed attempt kept public sector wage growth significantly below that of the private sector during 1996. After 1996, however, public sector real wages grew at an even faster pace than wages in the enterprise sector; a pattern that continued until early 2000. In sum, while over the 1991-1992 period, private sector wages grew 31 percent above wages in the public sector, opening a gap that continued wide open until 1996. Public sector wages started to catch up beginning in 1997, and by end-1999 the gap that emerged in 1991 was closed.[38] Efforts by the new Government to contain the wage bill, by reducing nominal wages by 5 percent in early 2000, achieved only partial success.

The recovery of wages in the public sector, without a parallel reduction in employment levels, has pushed the public sector wage bill to unprecedented levels expanding it by almost 6 percentage points of GDP since Source: de To1993. This trend and the overall level of the wage bill relative to GDP are not in line with that in any other Central and Eastern European country. At 12.4 percent of GDP, the room for savings by reducing the public sector wage bill seems large. However, despite the size of the public sector wage bill, there is relatively little knowledge in the country about key areas of public sector employment. The latest officially available data on public sector employment points to some 274,000 employees in the public sector (including employment in Defense and Police). This is equivalent to some 18 percent of total employment and to 6.1 percent of the country's population.

Reducing the public wage bill relative to GDP and aligning it with that in other transition countries will demand very restrictive compensation and recruitment policies, as well as civil service reform. The Government is aware of this challenge and has made the reduction of the wage bill a key component of its strategy to contain expenditures. As reflected in the government program to be supported by an IMF Stand-By Agreement, the Government plans to achieve a 10 percent nominal reduction in the CCG wage bill for the 2001 budget. Draft collective agreement among Croatian Employer's Association, the Government and several labor unions; if materialized, would keep the real wage bill for the civil and public services close to the level reached in 2001, throughout the 2002-03 period. This planned containment in labor costs is to take place through reductions in employment and wage moderation.[39] The celerity of the planned adjustments signals the Government awareness of the need to reduce the public sector wage bill as a matter of urgency.

---

[38] However, there is also evidence that the structure of wages is more compressed in the public sector than elsewhere; this should be considered at the time of implementing a public sector retrenchment in employment as it could lead to problems of adverse selection.

[39] Labor costs containment plans at the CG include the reduction of 10,000 employees in 2001, mainly from the ministries of Interior and Defense, the elimination of the meal allowance, the rationalization of the transportation allowance through an income test, and the reduction of overtime costs. In addition, the Government reduced the required noticed period for dismissal from 3-36 months to 6 months and the replacement rate for severance payments from 100 to 50 percent while it plans to harmonize wage categories across ministries through a new employment law on government officials.

Recommendations. The Government needs to focus both on public sector salary containment as well as on reducing the public sector labor force.[40] Our analysis shows that wages in the public sector are likely out of line with wages elsewhere in the economy. While government employment levels are, in general, not excessive, there is over-employment in certain areas of the public sector, e.g., Defense and Police. This report recommends that the Government of Croatia should:

- Maintain a freeze on salary levels in nominal terms throughout 2001;

- Reduce employment levels in those areas already identified as having excess employment (e.g., Defense and Police); and prepare specially crafted active labor market policies for adjusting military laid off personnel to civilian employment;

- In light of the Government's decentralization objectives, changes in employment at the local government (LG) level should be closely monitored; and any increase in employment at the LGs associated with the ongoing devolution of functions from the CG, should be linked to a parallel reduction of CG employment;

- Undertake a comprehensive review of the civil service and assign a separate government unit in charge of the rationalization of public sector employment.[41]

- This unit should have the authority to access information regarding employment at different levels of the public sector, including local governments. Creation of a unified database to cover all public sector employees should be a first step to enhance the knowledge of the public sector employment;

- Assess the current structure of employment according to the existing needs, identify areas of duplication, and design and carry out an employment rationalization plan;

- Identify services that could be contracted-out without affecting the quality of service provision and that could generate savings for the public sector;

- Strengthen monitoring over public enterprises' wage awarding. Given the links between raises in wages in public enterprises and the CG, efforts should be devoted to control wage increases in the public enterprises.

Non-wage Goods and Services

Croatia's public spending on non-wage goods and services has fallen substantially since the mid-1990s, and accounts now for about 11.2 percent of GDP (Figure 2.4). These expenditures include expenses for operations and maintenance, such as payments for the use of utility services, and non-wage spending on defense and police. In the Croatian chart of accounts, it also includes spending on social protection assistance, allowances for displaced persons, and the protection of war veterans and civil invalids of war, all of which are normally recorded as current transfers.

---

[40] Giving the existing links—at the time of negotiations—between wages within the CG and Public Enterprises, wage moderation should be also applied in the quasi-fiscal sector.

[41] Although currently different government bodies, such as the Department for State Administration under the Ministry of Justice, monitor a sub-set of the overall public sector human resources; there is no single administrative unit with an overall view of the public sector labor force.

Spending on non-wage goods and services has contracted sharply, by about 4.4 percentage points of GDP, since 1994. This contraction has raised concerns that operations and maintenance expenditures have borne the brunt of containment efforts at expenditure rationalization. Figure 2.5 shows, however, that the bulk of the contraction in this component has been in non-wage defense expenses, which have declined from 6.1 percent of GDP (1995) to 1.3 (2000) on an accrual basis. Social assistance expenses also fell by more than 0.7 percent of GDP since 1994, the result, on the one hand, of a reduction in the number of displaced persons, and on the other hand, of the transfer of some of the costs of social protection to local governments (starting from 1998). Civilian operations and maintenance expenditures, however, have remained fairly stable, as a percentage of GDP, throughout the whole period.

Figure 2.4: Expenditure for Goods and Services (% of GDP, accrual basis)

Source: Ministry of Finance and World Bank estimates.

Cuts in defense have been so far implemented through reductions in the non-wage component, and at 1.3 percent of GDP, it appears that the room for further savings in the non-wage component of Defense may be limited.[42] Spending on social assistance, at around 1 percent of GDP, is at its lowest level since 1994. This item is the best targeted social expenditure and, if anything, should be expanded at the expense of other social programs which are not targeted, or are not as well targeted.[43] Savings on non-wage goods and services should be the result of streamlined spending in operations and not at the expense of reduced allocations for maintenance. Identified needs for upgrading maintenance should come as a result of reallocation of funds from operations and investment.

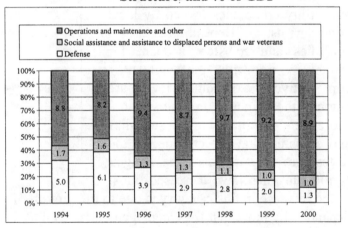

Figure 2.5: Purchases of Goods and Services, Structure and % of GDP

Source: Ministry of Finance and World Bank estimates.

---

[42] The analysis of the Defense sector later on in this Chapter, argues that having made substantial cuts in its non-wage outlays, the Defense sector needs now to reduce its wage bill so as to align its cost structure to Western-European standards.

[43] The demand for social assistance benefits may rise in the near future as many of those whom may loose their status of returnees and refugees may qualify for social assistance benefits.

Recommendations

- Identified needs for upgrading maintenance in sectors such as Transport, Health and Education, should be achieved by reallocating priorities from operations and new capital investments;[44]

- In light of the Government's decentralization objectives, the expansion of the maintenance costs in education, social protection and health sectors borne by LGs should be matched by an identical reduction at the CG level;

- Social assistance spending currently accounted for as "non-wage goods and services" should be properly accounted for under current transfers;

- Some maintenance and related administration costs could be saved by the sale of unused and unnecessary real estate owned by the state; specially by the Ministry of Defense.

Subsidies and Transfers

Subsidies and transfers include those transfers to EBFs (social security institutions), households, public enterprises, agriculture sector, banks and utility companies owned by local governments. Expenditures on subsidies and transfers account for roughly one-fifth of GDP—comparatively, expenditure levels are among the highest in the region. Moreover, as noted earlier, subsidies and transfers have been one of the fastest growing items in the budget. While subsidies have increased, most

Figure 2.6: Current Transfers of the Consolidated General Government (composition and as % of GDP)

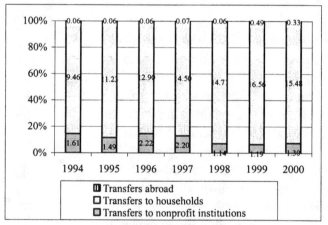

Source: Ministry of Finance and World Bank estimates.

of the increase in this category is due to the growth of current *transfers*. In fact, current transfers expanded by more than 7 percentage points of GDP from 1994 until 1999, only to recede by 1.1 percent of GDP in the year 2000; as a result, more than one third of all CGG expenditure and net lending is allocated to Subsidies and Transfers in 2000. In this way, all savings achieved in the area of Defense have been absorbed by increases in social transfers.[45]

Subsidies and transfers can be used for a number of different purposes: market failures, economies of scale in production, redistribution of income and alleviation of poverty. However,

---

[44] The Transport sector study carried out in the context of this PEIR, identifies the need to upgrade road maintenance by as much as 0.5 percent of GDP per year over a five year period.

[45] The 'peace dividend', resulting from the reduction in the military expenditure by itself, amounts to some 6.8 percentage points of GDP since 1995.

in Croatia it is difficult to evaluate if subsidies and transfers have achieved these objectives. To some extent subsidies and transfers are a consequence of the war, which led to extensive government involvement in housing, infrastructure and community reconstruction. In addition, the war also induced the Government to subsidize the operations of the Railway Company, which suffered significant losses from the destruction of several lines and a drastic decline in the number of passengers. The war also created the need to provide support for refugees, displaced persons and war veterans.[46] But, five years after the war, many subsidies and transfers remain.

Figure 2.7: Subsidies' Structure in 2000*

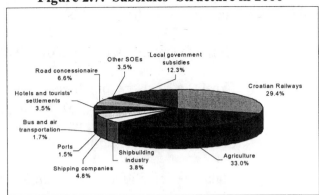

*Totaling 2.7% of GDP.
Source: Ministry of Finance and World Bank estimates.

Direct subsidies of the CGG amounted to 2.7 percent of GDP in 2000. Direct subsidies are fairly concentrated in transport (railways and the national airline) and agriculture. One third of the direct CCG subsidies goes to agriculture and almost one third to Croatian Railways (Figure 2.7). Local governments subsidize local utility companies for which there is no available detailed data. However, the level of budgetary subsidies is misleading as it excludes hidden subsidies given to shipyards, agro-combinates and other state-owned companies (Box 2.2). Other indirect subsidies also exist in the form of tax subsidies to war veterans and entities in the areas of special state concern. In many cases, direct and indirect subsidies have been used to postpone the resolution of different forms of enterprise crises, avoiding what otherwise would have resulted in bankruptcies and a healthy restructuring of the enterprise sector.

Box 2.2: Rehabilitation of Shipyards and Agro-Combinates

The 1995 Law on Rehabilitation of Selected Enterprises has defined measures for the rehabilitation of 14 majority state-owned companies, with the final aim of their privatization. Five out of 14 companies were shipyards whose rehabilitation costs reached some 2.3 percent of GDP in 2000 through: write-offs of claims on contributions and taxes, debt/equity swaps, loan reprogramming, issuance of guarantees on short-term liquidity loans and take over of debt towards foreign creditors. However, since 2001, the Government's assistance to shipyards has been carried out through the issuance of guarantees; while it also agreed to subsidize 8-10 percent of the value of all new ships, at an estimated cost of 0.25 percent of GDP per annum. In February 2001, the Government adopted a decision to rehabilitate majority state-owned agro-combinates amounting to around 1.4 percent of GDP. The state share in the overall cost is around 0.8 percent of GDP to be executed through different measures: write-offs of tax and contribution claims, recapitalization through cash injection, debt/equity swaps etc, while the rest is being borne by banks and suppliers.

Source: Croatia - Official Gazette

---

[46] The war had several other side effects with direct effect on the size of the public sector. In 1991, the country lost access to its share of the Federation's foreign exchange reserve (some US$5 billion), that was held by the National Bank of Yugoslavia. The Government assumed the banks debt with the domestic foreign currency depositors by issuing the so-called frozen foreign exchange bonds, which up until now represents the highest share of domestic debt, partially repaid through privatization of flats.

Recommendations. As the level and depth of subsidies in the economy are unknown, the Government needs, as a first step, to:

- Define/adopt a classification of subsidies according to EU standards;

- Create a registry of direct and indirect subsidies (such as custom waiver, contribution waiver, repayment of debts instead of final borrowers, tax waivers, guarantees called upon, tax concessions, credit lines with subsidized interest rates, debt/equity swaps, etc.)

- Make explicit all forms of subsidies and create a rationalization plan.

Current transfers have been the main factor behind the expansion of public spending. Current transfers grew by as much as 133 percent in real terms since 1994. In 2000, current transfers on an accrual basis stood at 17.1 percent of GDP. The expansion of current transfers has mostly arisen from the Pension and Health sectors.[47] Pensions currently absorb 72.5 percent of total CGG current transfers; sick pay and maternity allowances, an additional 10.4 percent, and child benefits take 4.5 percent. In addition to transfers to pensions and health, transfers to households also include transfers for child benefits, war veterans' allowances as well as other social transfers. There are also transfers to Bosnia and Herzegovina and to non-profit institutions.

The share of CG in current transfer payments has been increasing from 1.1 percent of GDP in 1994 to 9 percent in 1999 and 8.6 percent in 2000. However, most of the increase is a consequence of either changes in legislation[48] or government decisions to rehabilitate selected sectors or enterprises through payroll contribution waivers. The net result of these measures has been to make the EBFs more dependent on the CG budget. Since 2001 onward, CG additional transfers totaling 1.3 percent of GDP to the Pension Fund annually will be required by the Law on pensioners'

Figure 2.8: Structure of Current Transfers of Consolidated General Government (2000)*

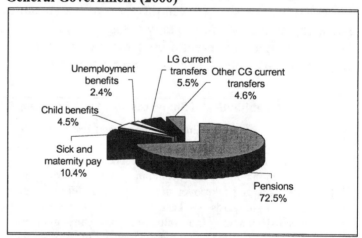

*Total amounts to 16.9% of GDP.
Source: Ministry of Finance and World Bank estimates.

debt restitution adopted by the Parliament in December 2000. Transfers to the pension and the health fund, and transfers for social assistance are discussed in more detail in Section C, along with specific recommendations for those expenditure areas.

---

[47] A more thorough treatment of these two sectors is carried out in Section C of this Chapter.
[48] These legislative changes include: the abolishment of the contributions to the child fund and the water management fund; as well as provisions contained in the so-called "small law" establishing the repayment of the special pension transfers.

Advances have been made in improving transparency regarding the recording of certain transfers; in particular, in handling Croatian transfers to the Federation of Bosnia and Herzegovina (FBiH). These transfers have been explicitly recognized in the budget since 1999. These transfers amounted to 0.5 percent of GDP in that year; of which 0.3 percent of GDP was allocated to fund the Croatian defense component, while the remaining 0.2 was transferred to war victims in the Federation of Bosnia and Herzegovina. Transfers to FBiH receded to 0.3 percent of GDP in 2000.

The Functional Composition of Expenditures of the Consolidated Central Government

As noted earlier, the trend in CCG[49] expenditures over the 1991—1999 period can be broken into two clearly different sub-periods (Table 2.3). From Independence to the end of the 1991-1995 war, defense and, to a lesser extent, housing, accounted for most of the expansion. Expenditures on social security and welfare affairs, the bulk of which are pension expenditures, on the other hand, contracted during this period. This situation reversed in 1996—1999: with the end of the war (1995) outlays for defense started to fall, and outlays for social security started to recover, growing rapidly beginning in 1995, and consuming most of the "peace dividend" coming from the reduction in defense. This section examines the trends in the main components of sectoral spending—pensions, health, education, social assistance and child allowances, transport and defense. The first five categories alone account for more than one quarter of GDP and constitute the largest component of the CCG budget, representing 65.1 percent of total expenditures. They are also critical to the social well being of a large majority of the population, so any expenditure rationalization in these sectors must be done only after considerable analysis and consultation. In this regard, the overall poverty impact of social spending is poor, as little social spending actually reached the poor (Box 2.5). Defense and police expenditures have been declining, but still remain large (nearly 13 percent of total expenditures), and transport expenditures are also large in the CCG budget and include subsidies of a number of transport activities and guarantees for large transport projects. These sectoral analyses raise some important issues regarding spending in these areas, and put forward some recommendations regarding policy reforms. However, expenditure rationalization should not focus exclusively on these sectors. This analysis illustrates the kind of analysis that needs to be undertaken for all parts of the budget to achieve a comprehensive reform of public finance.

---

[49] We switch to the Consolidated **Central** Government as a unit of analysis for the study of the functional classification of expenditure since there is no reporting on expenditures by functions at the level of the CGG.

Table 2.3: Consolidated Central Government Expenditure by Function (1991–2000) Accrual Basis

% of GDP	1991	1992	1993	1994	1995	1996	1997	1998	1999	2000
Total expenditure	37.6	38.6	37.4	40.2	44.7	46.3	45.6	48.0	50.4	43.9
General public services	0.8	0.8	1.0	1.6	1.8	1.7	1.5	2.2	1.9	1.6
Defense affairs and services	4.9	7.0	7.8	8.1	9.4	6.8	5.5	5.0	3.3	2.9
Public order and safety affairs	3.1	2.1	2.3	2.9	3.0	3.0	3.1	2.8	2.8	2.7
Education affairs and services	2.9	1.8	1.8	2.9	2.9	2.9	3.0	3.0	3.6	3.6
Health affairs and services	6.1	6.3	5.9	5.3	6.6	7.8	7.1	7.5	7.2	6.7
Social security and welfare services	14.7	11.7	11.7	12.2	13.4	14.5	16.2	16.8	18.8	18.2
Housing and community services	0.3	0.7	0.5	1.1	2.1	3.3	2.7	2.9	2.3	1.6
Recreational, cultural and religious affairs	0.4	0.3	0.3	0.3	0.4	0.4	0.4	0.4	0.6	0.6
Fuel and energy affairs and services	0.0	0.0	0.0	0.0	0.0	0.0	0.0	0.0	0.0	0.0
Agriculture, forestry, fishing, and hunting	0.4	1.6	1.3	0.7	0.5	0.5	0.5	1.0	0.9	1.0
Mining, manufacturing & construction	0.0	0.0	0.2	0.2	0.3	0.4	0.5	0.4	0.5	0.5
Transport & communication	2.4	2.5	2.5	2.8	2.2	3.1	2.8	3.0	3.7	3.2
Other economic affairs and services	1.0	1.1	0.9	0.3	0.2	0.3	0.4	0.4	0.5	0.5
Exp. not classified by major group	0.8	2.7	1.2	1.6	1.8	1.6	2.0	2.5	4.2	0.8
Memo items:										
Defense and Public order: (2)+(3)	7.9	9.2	10.1	11.0	12.4	9.9	8.5	7.9	6.1	5.6
Social spending: (4)+(5)+(6)	23.8	19.9	19.4	20.5	23.0	25.2	26.3	27.3	29.6	28.6

Source: "Government Finance Statistics", IMF up until 1997; Ministry of Finance and authors' estimates afterwards.

Box 2.3: Social Sector Spending: Is the Poverty Impact Adequate?

Public sector social spending in Croatia is high in comparison with regional economies (Figure 2.9). In fact, when the costs of the administration have been subtracted from total social spending, all layers of the Government spent some 26 percent of GDP on social programs in 2000,[1] an amount equivalent to 49.5 percent of total expenditures.[2] Figure 2.9 shows that it is health and to a lesser extent social transfers (including pensions), where Croatia's spending as a share of GDP more clearly exceeds the comparators. However, despite these high levels of spending, the effect of social spending on poverty alleviation is relatively low. One of the two main causes of poverty—together with lack of employment opportunities—is the inadequacy of the social safety net (World Bank, 2001).

Figure 2.9 Functional Allocation of Spending (1997)

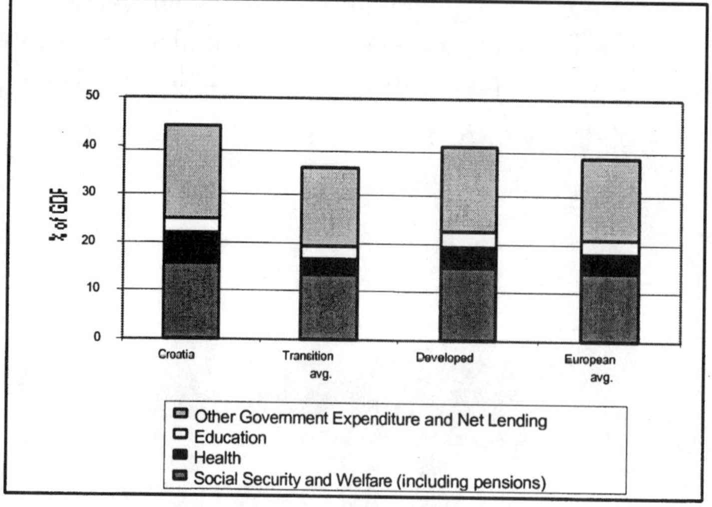

Source: Ministry of Finance and staff calculations.

1. Education, unemployment, social protection, pensions, health care and war-related expenditures including reconstruction.
2. The total cost of all social special programs, including salaries of the public employees who administer these programs, was around 36 percent of GDP.

Box 2.3 (continued)

Social programs achieve little real redistribution and contribute little to reduce poverty, despite spending over one fourth of GDP. Spending on social programs, primarily health and pensions (and especially early retirement) is not well targeted to the poor (Table 2.4). On the other hand, social transfers, which are better targeted, have a much lower share in overall spending. [3]

Table 2.4: Social Spending (% of GDP)

	How much the government spends on social programs?	How much the poorest 20% of population receive?	How much the poorest 8.4% of population receive?
Pensions	12	1.9	0.7
Social Assistance	0.4	0.2	0.1
Child & Family Allowance	1.4	0.3	0.1
Unemployment benefit	0.4	0.2	0.1
All transfers	**17**	**2.8**	**1.0**
Education spending	3	0.5	0.2
Healthcare (estimate)	7	0.4	0.2
Total social spending	**27**	**3.7**	**1.4**

Source: World Bank 2001.

It is estimated that the poorest 8.4 percent of the population receive only 2.8 percent of public health spending and 6 percent of total spending on education; making the provision of these services clearly regressive (World Bank, 2001). Although, the poor are not excluded from the system, those who are relatively well off benefit the most.

In the area of pensions, the report finds that in 1998, 47 percent of the pensioners received benefits lower than 1000 HRK per month;[4] and that more than one fourth of the people 60 years old and older did not receive any benefit. The poverty profile identified those elderly excluded from the pension system or receiving low pensions as particularly vulnerable to poverty, constituting the largest group among the poor. In summary, the overall impact of social services financed by the Government is definitely regressive. Even the relative allocation of funds among targeted cash-transfer programs is not effective in reducing poverty, as the better targeted programs, such as Social Assistance, receive less than one third of the funding of less well targeted programs such as Child Allowance.

----

3. The concentration coefficient for total transfers is positive, showing that in fact instead of reducing inequality, they enhance it.
4. The national poverty line, for a single person, estimated in that report was equivalent to some HRK1290 per month. In 2001, after the restitution payment adjustment, 20 percent of pensioners remained below the absolute poverty line.

Health

Health expenditures are usually correlated with income levels and health indicators such as life expectancy. From an economic point of view, an adequate provision of health care improves human capital by strengthening an individual's capacity to work productively. The rationale for providing public health care rests on the argument that certain health services have public goods characteristics, such as disease control and health education. Other health services provide positive externalities as benefits arise beyond the direct beneficiaries, such as immunization against infectious diseases. These types of services are called primary care. To the extent that health care financed through the budget is used to provide primary care with public goods characteristics, then public expenditure in health is allocated efficiently.

Overview and issues. Health expenditures in Croatia relative to GDP are above the average for European countries and have been increasing over time. Yet, patients and providers remain dissatisfied with the levels and quality of health services. Health care spending has been growing faster than GDP. In 2000, total health spending (public and private) represented more than 9 percent of GDP, of which 7.0 percent of GDP is public spending on health (both unconsolidated figures), financed by the Croatian Health Insurance Institute (CHII). An additional 1.7 percent of GDP is transferred to the CHII from the CG, for the purpose of financing non-health expenses, such as sick and maternity leave benefits, equipment for newborn children and other expenditure.[50] These levels of public health spending are far above those in many European countries, where the average public spending on health stands at about 4 percent of GDP. However, increasing costs, decreasing numbers of health insurance contributors (resulting in part from rising unemployment), and substantial contribution exemptions have led to significant deficits and payment arrears in the health sector.

The measures undertaken so far to contain costs and improve efficiency (e.g., hard budget caps for hospitals and co-payment for drugs, etc.) have produced some positive results. However, these reforms are not sufficiently comprehensive to advance systemic changes and eliminate distortions in the existing incentives that affect delivery of health services. Left unchanged, these incentives will perpetuate socially sub-optimal behavior of patients and providers and, ultimately, undermine the fiscal sustainability of the system.

For example, a recent reform has introduced capitation methods in primary health care provider payments to improve incentives for more efficient and effective care. Capitation contracts with primary health providers include provisions intended to limit the use of expensive specialists and hospital care. However, the loopholes in the new system make it possible for patients and providers to bypass the system and obtain unnecessary referrals. As a result, patients continue to *overuse specialist and hospital care*. Similarly, the existing payment system for hospitals, based on the cost of delivered services, encourages over-supply and lacks incentives for cost-containment. Alternative *prospective payment systems (such as Diagnostic Related Groups)* may provide better incentives for the hospitals to improve resource use and efficiency in production of health services. Reduced rates of hospital and specialist care utilization would translate into significant savings for the health system. It is estimated that a 10 percent reduction in hospital and specialist health care utilization will decrease total health sector expenditures by about 4.2 percent.

Financing. Health care in Croatia is financed mainly by the Croatian Health Insurance Institute (CHII). Other sources of funding include budgetary transfers from the Government, co-payments, informal payments by patients, and payments from other insurance companies. Roughly 90 percent of the total health system is financed by the CHII or by government transfers received through the CHII, with the remaining 10 percent provided through private insurance companies and private payments. Of the total CHII revenues for 1999, roughly 80 percent came from payroll contributions, 19 percent from government transfers, and 1 percent from other sources, mainly co-payments. Payroll contributions to the CHII are currently set at 16 percent of gross wages (7 percent from employers and 9 percent from employees). Receipts from payroll

---

[50] These other non-health expenses include: funeral cost reimbursement, compensations for work-related accidents, family member care and paid leave due to pregnancy complications.

contributions have been affected by decreasing levels of employment, the growing informalization of the economy, and an increasing share of contributors who are either eligible to contribute at minimum levels or are fully exempt. In addition, in their effort to promote job growth, the Government reduced the rate of employers' payroll contribution in mid-2000 from 9 percent to 7 percent, which further affected CHII's revenues.

The system is also affected by low co-payment rates[51] and a broad range of exemptions that reduce the number of contributors[52] and patients who pay co-payments for health services. Currently, about 30 percent of the population pay contributions, and only 20 percent are subject to co-payments. Co-payments, which in other European countries are a significant source of revenues (about 7-10 percent of total health revenues), represent less than 1 percent of total revenues in Croatia. Government transfers, the second most important source of financing, are intended to cover benefits such as extended maternity leave, health insurance of unemployed and uninsured, as well as certain type of equipment. Throughout 1998-1999, the Government transferred an additional 0.4 percent and 0.8 percent of GDP for debt settlement towards suppliers.[53]

Expenditures. CHII total spending has increased from 6.5 percent of GDP in 1994, the year following the first important reform in the system, to 9.3 percent in 2000. This increase was accompanied by a growth in arrears equivalent to approximately 1 percent of GDP per year, and deficits. Rising costs in health care are attributed mainly to wage increases in the health sector that outpaced the growth of average wages in the rest of the economy, as well as to increasing costs of a national sick leave program.

The sick leave program in Croatia is pretty generous. In fact, after the first 42 days of sick leave (paid by the employer), beneficiaries are entitled to up to one year of sick leave, covered by the CHII. Up until early 2001, the replacement rate was 80 percent up to six months and 90 percent afterwards up to one year and could even reach 100 percent in certain cases. Proposed changes aimed at lowering the replacement rate from 80 to 70 percent, while preserving the full replacement for special cases (such as occupational- related sickness, pregnancy complications, work-place accidents, etc.) are still pending to be implemented. Anecdotal evidence points to a widespread misuse of sick leaves by enterprises as a way to temporarily hide redundant employment.[54]

Efficiency. Even though the health system is dominated by more expensive secondary and tertiary care, higher CHII spending on hospital care than for primary care is not unusual and the numbers themselves are not a major cause for concern. What is worrisome, however, is the trend of public expenditures over time. This trend exhibits a shift from primary care towards the

---

[51] Co-payments are paid as a lump sum per prescription for drugs or per visit to GP or specialist. They range basically from US$0.7 to US$2.5, rarely reaching US$6 for special medical procedures. The co-payment for one of the most expensive special medical procedures –the MRI- is less than US$15.

[52] Among the groups exempted from making co-payments are: pensioners, war veterans, war invalids and their families, refugees, returnees, unemployed, children and students.

[53] These special transfers were linked in part to the Government's decision to revive some companies by paying their accumulated arrears with the CHII for unpaid contributions.

[54] Health costs were also affected by an erratic tax policy that introduced the VAT for drugs and medical products in 1998, and removed it 23 months later selectively for drugs and medical disability equipment from the CHII's list.

hospital and specialist health care. In fact, while the share of primary care declined over time from some 23 percent to around 19 percent of core health expenditures financed by CHII, the share of hospital and specialist health care expenditures increased from 51.7 percent in 1994 to 58.5 percent in 1999. Within the category of secondary health care, public expenditures have been on the rise in recent years in both hospital care as well as polyclinic specialist care.

Scope for private sector intervention. Croatia is accustomed to a high public sector participation in health. However, the transition to private practice at the level of GPs initiated in 1993 has proven effective and has been relatively swift and successful. There is a broader scope of private sector participation in primary care, particularly for diagnostic services and outpatient specialist care. Private sector involvement should also be encouraged in hospital care, particularly for low-intensity services (minor surgeries, deliveries, etc.) and long-term care. Presently, there is only one private hospital in Croatia. However, given the size of the market, there should be ample scope for further private involvement in this area of health sector production and delivery. Underutilized hospital facilities in the public sector could be used for encouraging private sector initiatives.

Recommendations. *Short-Term Measures*

- Increase patient co-payments for the services of primary health care institutions, hospitals and pharmacies. Experience of other countries indicates that co-payments at 'appropriate' levels can potentially drive down frivolous use of health care and contribute to shifting utilization from expensive specialists services to less cost-intensive primary care.

- Decrease significantly the share of population exempted from co-payments. Currently, 80 percent of the Croatian people, most of whom are non-poor, are exempted from making any co-payments. This number is too high and dilutes the policy impact of co-payments. It is suggested that co-payment exemptions should apply only to children, unemployed and those receiving targeted social assistance, collectively equal to less than 50 percent of the population.

- Introduce reference pricing for medical supplies. Reference pricing was planned to be introduced for pharmaceuticals in 1999, and over 1,300 drugs covered fully or partially under insurance were included in the reference list. A similar reference list should also be prepared for medical supplies so as to rationalize procurement and contain costs.

- Impose an immediate freeze of the wage bill. Wages and salaries represent over 50 percent of health revenues of the Croatian Health Insurance Institute and constitute the single-largest item of expenditure.

Long-Term Measures

- Introduce Diagnosis-Related Group system. International experience demonstrates the cost-savings that result from prospective payments systems, the most widely used of which is the Diagnosis-Related Group system (DRGs). Starting with the implementation of already defined protocols (10-15) for the most frequent diagnosis, further DRGs should be developed using costs and utilization numbers from different service centers in Croatia. In the initial stages, expected savings need not be significant, considering that the DRGs would be priced on existing levels of costs of services; however, this would provide the appropriate incentives for health facilities to contain costs and rationalize provision of services. At the same time, control over the system should be strengthened to avoid a potential misuse of DRGs, by drifting away from properly priced diagnosis.

- Reduce reimbursement levels for funeral expenses, traveling expenses, transportation costs. Presently, these add up to around 0.1 percent of GDP, and represent a potential source of savings. In any case, these expenditures are more social welfare type expenditures, and should therefore be financed through other means, not through health insurance.

- Reduce transfers from health insurance to households in the form of sick pay, maternity benefits, etc. Currently, the CHII pays transfers to households for sick-leaves, accidents at work, care for family members when ill, pregnancy complications and maternity leaves, collectively accounting for over 19 percent of all CHII expenditures (2000). With the exception of additional maternity leave and equipment for newborn children, which are paid for by the state and only routed through the CHII, all other allowances are paid out of CHII funds. Since these expenditures do not constitute health care expenditures, they should be either financed through other means, such as social welfare finance for maternity leaves, or cut in the level and duration. The maximum period of sick leave should be reduced to six months, while the assessment procedure for extended sick leave eligibility should be strengthened. This will cause significant saving in health-related expenditures.

Pensions

Increasing outlays and deficits of the pension system have raised concerns regarding the system's sustainability. The pension system currently absorbs close to 6 percent of GDP in government transfers, and it will require an additional 0.6 to 0.7 percentage point of GDP in the coming year 2002. Unfavorable demographic trends, the war, and transitional recession, all combined to reduce the financial viability of the pension system in Croatia. The use of pensions as a social cushion for lay-offs, and the entry of new categories of disabled and survivors' defenders from the 1991-1995 war, have resulted in a dramatic expansion in the share of pension benefits to GDP. In parallel, efforts to reduce replacement rates have been successfully confronted by the powerful lobby of pensioners.

Croatia has adopted (1998) an ambitious pension reform that is in the process of transforming the current pay-as-you-go system into a financially viable multi-pillar system. However, it will take 20 more years for the contributory component to regain balance while the overall system, including the non-contributory component, will still be in deficit by the year 2020 (a deficit equivalent to about 1.2 percent of GDP). In the short-term, however, transition

costs, especially related to the second
tier, will require additional funding.
Therefore, tight control and further
reforms to both the contributory and
non-contributory system are needed
to resolve the current fiscal crisis.

The equity dimension of the
pension system in Croatia is not
bright either. In fact, despite spending
more than 13 percent of GDP, of
which more than forty percent is
financed by general government
resources (through CG transfers), the
Croatian pension system does very
little to reduce poverty among the
elderly, as benefits among different
groups of pensioners are excessively
disparate. Extremely low minimum
pensions and the existence of groups
of privileged beneficiaries contribute to this outcome.[55]

Box 2.4: The Current Pension System

The pension system in Croatia is currently a pay-as-you-go
system operated by a Pension fund, which is the result of the
merger of the Workers Fund, the Agriculture Fund and the Self-
employment Fund, integrated into the Pension Fund from January
1999. The system collects revenues from three sources:

- **Payroll contributions** of 19.5 percent on gross wages: 8.75
  percent from employers and 10.75 percent from employees;
- **CG transfers**, to cover for beneficiaries whose benefits are
  provided by special laws and not covered by adequate
  contributions during their active years. Among them are: war
  veterans, military and police personnel, parliamentarians and
  other special occupations. In addition, CG covers through
  transfers the loss in PF revenues form the payroll tax cut
  established in 2000, matching contributions for farmers and
  in practice any residual deficit that may arise;
- **Dividends** on the Pension Fund's portfolio obtained in the
  privatization process.

The system will add a second pillar, which will start operations in
January 2002.

Table 2.5 : Sources of Budget Obligations – Moderate Wage Growth Scenario (% of GDP)

	1999	2000	2001	2002	2003	2004	2005	2010
Pension Institute Total Revenues	8.7	8.3	7.9	6.3	5.9	5.6	5.3	5.6
Pension Institute Total Expenditures	13.3	12.9	13.7	12.9	11.2	10.8	10.3	8.7
Pension Institute Financing Gap	**-4.6**	**-4.6**	**-5.8**	**-6.5**	**-5.3**	**-5.2**	**-5.0**	**-3.1**
Gross Aggregate Budget Transfers	**4.6**	**4.6**	**5.8**	**6.5**	**5.3**	**5.2**	**5.0**	**3.1**
Of which:								
Non-contributory pension rights	**2.2**	**2.1**	**2.0**	**2.0**	**1.9**	**1.8**	**1.8**	**1.5**
Army, Defenders, Police	1.2	1.4	1.3	1.3	1.3	1.3	1.3	1.1
WWII pension beneficiaries	0.4	0.3	0.3	0.3	0.3	0.2	0.2	0.2
Other Special Pensions	0.6	0.4	0.4	0.4	0.3	0.3	0.3	0.2
Contributory system	**2.0**	**2.1**	**3.3**	**4.3**	**3.2**	**3.1**	**2.9**	**1.3**
First pillar	0.9	1.0	1.0	0.9	0.8	0.8	0.7	-0.8
Restitution payments	1.1	1.1	2.3	2.1	1.1	1.0	0.9	0.6
Gross transition costs*				*1.3*	*1.3*	*1.3*	*1.3*	*1.5*
Administrative costs net of non- tax revenues	**0.4**	**0.4**	**0.5**	**0.2**	**0.2**	**0.3**	**0.3**	**0.3**

*Net transition cost would be equal the flow of 1st pillar contributions to 2nd pillar funds minus projected parametric PAYG
savings.
Source: Bank staff estimates (minus sign means surplus).

---

[55] In addition, more than one third of the persons age 60 and older, do not receive any pension benefits.

Financing needs. The pension system is a major source of fiscal strain. Since 1990, pension benefits have swollen from 10 to almost 13 percent of GDP and are estimated to reach almost 14 percent of GDP in 2001. Although pension earmarked payroll taxes, at 19.5 percent on gross earnings, are relatively high by international standards, revenues from contributions barely cover sixty percent of the current spending on pensions. The remaining financing gap is covered by the State Budget. CG transfers to the Pension Fund are estimated to reach close to 6 percent of GDP by 2001.

Recent developments. Over the past decade, contributors have dropped by about 800,000 persons while Pension Institute revenues have shrunk to about 8.3 percent of GDP in 2000. At the same time the Government used the pension system as a social cushion to compensate for limited employment opportunities. Generous early retirement policies and low standard retirement ages have led to a large increase in the number of beneficiaries. Today, excluding military and war veterans and pensions paid abroad, there are about 980,000 pensioners. These developments, common to most pension systems in transition economies, have been aggravated in Croatia by the 1991-1995 war and the strong resistance of pensioners' associations to government attempts to slow down benefit increases. New types of high benefits with relatively loose eligibility criteria were introduced for war veterans and their families and procedures that resulted in approximately 1 percent of GDP of additional expenditures per annum. At the same time, the Constitutional Court ruled in favor of pensioners' associations that had challenged government policies to compress replacement rates and price indexing benefits. As a result, since 1998, restitution payments have been introduced, which have contributed to expand pension expenditures by an additional one percent of GDP in 1999, and will further increase them again by an additional 1.2 percent of GDP this year.

Short-term prospects. The 1998 reform of the contributory system will, in the medium-term, reverse these deteriorating trends. In the short run, however, it will also increase the fiscal burden. The creation of private pension funds in 2002 will generate an additional shortfall in the Pension Institute revenues of about 1.3 percent of GDP. At that time, the whole system financing gap could reach 6.5 percent of GDP. In the medium and long term, savings from increased retirement age and reduced replacement rates in the first pillar will gradually reduce the size of the contributory part of the system. However, the additional payments related to the Constitutional court ruling will delay the date at which the public pillar would no longer require funding from the CG to at least the year 2015.

Box 2.5: The New Pension Law

The new law modifies the current pension system in a way that should bring some savings to the Pension Fund:

- Retirement ages were originally (1998) 55 for women and 60 for men and are being progressively brought to 60 and 65, respectively, at the rate of an additional six months contribution period per calendar year
- The calculation formula for pension benefits takes into account the 10 best paid years of the beneficiary but will progressively move to encompass his or her whole lifetime earnings
- In line with the provisions contained in the new Law on Pension Insurance, the early retirement age is being raised from 50 to 55 for women and from 60 to 65 for men and the decrement for early retirement has been increased
- As a result of the new law, the adjustment and indexation of benefits were converted from full price indexation, to the currently applied "Swiss formula" – an average of the increases between cost of living and wages.

Source: Croatia – Official Gazette

Short-term trends in expenditures could further deteriorate if either the Government fails to resist interest group pressures or attempts to move employees out of the public payroll by granting special early retirement provisions. The potential costs of some of these actions are assessed below. Based on simulations run in a 5 years horizon, pension costs could increase if the Government:

- Fails to stop the flow of new war invalids and defenders and starts granting early retirement privileges to relieve the social cost associated to the retrenchment of some 20,000 to 30,000 employees from the Ministries of Defense and Internal Affairs. This will increase pension expenditures by 0.6-0.9 percent of GDP;

- Maintains unclear links between contributions and entitlements in the enterprises being restructured or at the edge of bankruptcy; or applies loose control on how disability benefits are granted after long sick leaves. These could open the door to a new surge in early retirement and an uncontrolled increase in disability benefits, that will increase pension expenditures by an additional 0.9 percent of GDP;

- Fails to raise currently low compliance among farmers and the self-employed and fails to adjust their minimum taxable income to reflect nominal wage growth. This will decrease Pension Institute revenues by an additional 0.3 percent of GDP.

Equity. Despite the current high levels of both absolute spending on pensions and budgetary transfers to the system, the Croatian pension system is not effective in reducing poverty among elderly. On one hand, more than one third of the population age 60 and older did not receive any benefits from the system in 1998 (The World Bank, 2000b). For half of those who did receive a pension; their monthly benefits were below HRK 1000, i.e., below the absolute poverty level.[56] This situation was partially reverted as only 20 percent of those receiving pensions in 2001 were below the absolute poverty line, the result in turn of increase in benefits arising from the aforementioned Constitutional Court ruling. At the other extreme, defender's disability pensions are on average 3.5 time higher than civilian benefits, while defender's survivor benefits are 5 times higher.

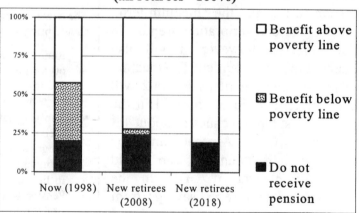

Figure 2.10: Pension Reform and Poverty among Retirees (all retirees =100%)*

*Total number of retirees is the sum of elderly (over 60 years) and disabled individuals. Poverty line is constant in real terms and set at 1000 HRK per month per capita in 1998.
Source: Castel (2000a).

---

[56] As defined in World Bank 2001.

Although the new pension reform will not eliminate the inequities generated by the existence of privileged pension groups; it will improve the situation of those at the bottom of the pension distribution. The combination of new indexing rules (50 percent wages and 50 percent prices) and the setting of a new minimum benefit per year of service, will combine to eliminate poverty almost completely among those covered by the system. System projections indicate that only about 2 percent of the workers who will retire over 1999-2008 and only 1 percent of those retiring over 2009-2018, will be below the poverty line (Figure 2.10).[57] However, the new eligibility criteria will only slightly reduce the share of those who do not receive benefits. Simulations that combine this small expansion in the number of eligible beneficiaries with the expected increases in minimum pensions show that the share of the elderly that either do not receive a pension, or receive a pension below the poverty line will drop from almost two thirds in 1998, to about 30 percent by the year 2008. This share will further shrink to 20 percent by 2018. In summary, the implementation of the pension reform will be a major step towards reducing poverty among the elderly.

Recommendations. The Government must take an active role in containing pension expenditures in general and merit pensions in particular, as well as enhancing the contribution base in order to reduce the short-term fiscal burden of the pension system. A list of possible actions is presented below. The first set of measures is aimed at reforming the non-contributory component of the system, while the second mostly aims at deepening the changes in the contributory system introduced by the 1998 Pension Law.

Non-contributory component

- Support Ministry of Veterans Affairs in tightening eligibility rules and control procedures in granting defenders disability pensions;

- Revise defenders pension benefits system, especially survivors' pensions ;

- Harmonize benefits levels between civilian, military, police and defenders;

- Avoid using early retirement for public employment retrenchment in general and, in particular, minimize the use of privileged early retirement for employees of the Ministries of Defense and Internal Affairs (by Presidential decree).

Contributory component

- Refrain from any further cut in contribution rates until the system shows clear financial improvement;

- Maintain tight control procedures for granting general disability benefits;

---

[57] An additional 4 percent of workers might find that their wages, and therefore contributions, were too low to be eligible under the new rules for a pension; they are mainly women who have very short or disrupted working careers or low earnings.

- Reduce early retirement options: (i) cut the minimum pension per year of service for those who remain exclusively within the first pillar (i.e., reduce accrual rate to one more consistent with actuarial principles); (ii) raise the annual penalty for early retirement in the first pillar from the present level to around 5 percent (which is closer to an actuarially neutral adjustment); and (iii) introduce the same annual decrement for early retirees on the minimum pension as the one for other pensioners;

- Eliminate exemptions on contributions and stop the rehabilitation of enterprises through payroll contribution waivers;

- Privatize the remaining asset holdings of the PI;

- Increase contribution compliance among farmers and self-employed and index farmers and self-employed minimum taxable base to wage growth;

- Finalize the unification of the personal income, pension and health contribution base and accelerate the full establishment of the Central Registry of Affiliates (REGOS);

- Transfer wage and service recording system from Pension Institute to the Central Registry of Affiliates (REGOS);

- Unify the contribution rate for employers and employees according to the European Social Charter;

- Eliminate the preferential treatment of pensioners in the area of personal income tax by making the nontaxable bracket for pensioners equal to that for workers;[58]

- Consider a temporary increase of the share of the new private pension funds' public titles investment requirement.

Further delays in the creation of the individual accounts[59] will be inconsistent with the reform of the system and could jeopardize the long-term financial improvement of the contributory component (Figure 2.10). The current transition relies on the principle that the gradual decrease in public pillar benefits must be offset by the gradual increase of private annuities from the mandatory second pillar. Any change in such policy would appear unfair to current contributors, be subject to legal challenges, and possibly derail the pension reform. Moreover, as mentioned above, contribution compliance is a serious problem. The creation of the Central Registry of Affiliates (REGOS) with the maintenance of individual accounts is essential for establishing reliable individual records and improving the functioning of both the first and the second pillar; thereby, lessening the fiscal burden of the system.

---

[58] At the moment the tax-exempted part of pensioners' income is twice as high as that for workers (1,250 HRK for workers and 2,500 HRK for pensioners).

[59] Currently planned to take place by January 2002.

Figure 2.11 presents the expected trends in the deficits of both the non-contributory and contributory system. These trends clearly show that the financial position of the contributory component is expected to steadily improve after 2003. By contrast, without reform, the fiscal burden of the non-contributory component is expected to decline at a very slow pace.

Education

The most important challenge for the education sector in Croatia is to modernize it, making it suitable to provide the type of skills and knowledge required by the global economy. Croatia needs to reform the curriculum by focusing on general skills and abilities valued by the market economy, adding more flexibility to the education system to make it more adaptable to the current changing environment. Unlike the other social sectors analyzed above, Croatia is not overspending on education relative to other

Figure 2.11: Sources of Pension Financing Gap (% of GDP)

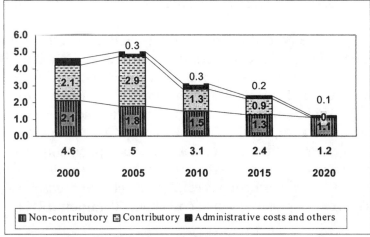

Source: Staff estimates.

countries in the region. Croatia's public spending on education measured both as a share of GDP and as a percent of total public expenditure is below OECD averages. However, the Education sector needs to overhaul the output it provides. The implementation of the necessary reforms will require substantial sector investments.

Not only does the sector need to overhaul the type of product that it currently delivers, but also it needs to make quality education more broadly accessible to the poorest segments of the population, thus contributing to make the system more equitable. The recent World Bank Poverty Report for Croatia finds lack of education to be one of the most important determinants of poverty and unemployment. The study finds relatively high returns to education in Croatia, which, combined with a relatively wide spread of education achievements,[60] contributes to highly inequitable outcomes. This indicates a stratified education system that fails to operate as a mechanism for social mobility. Access to upper level secondary school, and even more so, to higher education, is severely limited. As a result, for every HRK spent on tertiary education per person in the lowest quintile, the state spends more than 6 HRK per person in the top quintile. Public expenditure in education is poverty-neutral at the primary level, is biased against the poorest quintile at the secondary level and strongly biased against the poor at the tertiary level. At the secondary level the wealthiest quintile has enrollment rates 17 percentage points higher than the poorest quintile. At the tertiary level the wealthiest quintile has six times the enrollment rate of the poorest quintile.

---

[60] The standard deviation for years of schooling for the Croatian population over 25 years old is 4.2 (with mean 9.5) higher than in Argentina and Uruguay and significantly higher than in Europe.

Besides changing the type of output it provides and providing better access to the poorest segment of the population, the sector would benefit from changing the input mix. There are important issues in the way resources are allocated within the sector and across sub-sectors. On one hand, relatively few resources are assigned for non-staff inputs, especially for school maintenance and budget items that directly affect student learning. On the other hand, intra-sectoral allocations are not in line with OECD's. Croatia allocates a higher proportion of its total spending on education to preschool and a lower share to secondary education relative to OECD. In addition, the norms that all institutions of education are required to use for budgeting may result in inefficiencies. Student/teacher ratios are declining below OECD ratios, especially for secondary education, while tertiary education has serious internal efficiency problems.

The cost of reforming the system may be high. It is not clear how much it will cost to modernize primary and secondary education, but the bill will be much bigger than that for modernizing higher education. Both the Ministry of Education and Sports (MOES) and the Ministry of Science and Technology (MST) have proposed reforms of the sector. However, neither ministry has evaluated the fiscal implications of their ideas. For example, the MOES has proposed defining the final year of preschool and 9th grade as compulsory. Using 1998/99 enrollments of five year olds in preschool, population estimates[61] for the five year old cohort and recurrent unit costs for preschool in that year (excluding the investment or rental costs of adding over 10,000 preschool places); the preschool proposal may cost up to 95 million HRK per year. The grade 9 proposal would cost about 40 million HRK per year.

Financing. As noted above, relative to OECD norms, Croatia's spending on education is moderate both as a percent of GDP and as share of total public expenditure. While average education spending for OECD countries stands at 5.5 percent of GDP, or 14 percent of the total public expenditure (1997 data), Croatia spent a moderate 4.3 percent of GDP, or 8.3 percent of total CGG expenditure on accrual basis, in 2000. School-level budgets betray skimpy budgets for supplies and maintenance. More important, they show serious shortfalls or virtually no funding for expenditures that affect student learning: the professional development of teachers; computer, science, and language laboratories; the modern equipment needed in vocational/technical programs to position students to enter the labor force; or libraries that can sustain independent student work.

Unit cost for preschool relative to unit cost for basic education in Croatia is higher than in OECD, signaling potential inefficiencies at preschool level. In contrast, Croatia appears to be underspending at the secondary level relative to OECD ratios, even though student/teacher ratios are declining and staff costs as a percent of total recurrent costs are increasing. For primary and secondary education, it spends only half the OECD share for non-staff recurrent expenses.

Data on private financing of education are too incomplete to calculate estimates of total public and private expenditures on education in Croatia. There is also evidence of a very limited private provision. There are private payments and cost recovery for publicly provided services at

---

[61] Population estimates come from Andelko Akrap and Jakov Gelo (1999), "Demographic research in Croatia, first phase of the project: Estimate of population in Croatia in 1998 according to sex and age structure". Faculty of Economics: University of Zagreb. Using official population estimates would increase the estimated cost of these two proposals.

each level of education. Parents pay fees for preschool, although it is impossible to estimate the total private costs at this level of education because the percent of cost recovery is set by the town/municipality and varies across the 542 towns and municipalities. In primary and secondary education, parents pay for school supplies, textbooks, and, if students have to take public transport to school, for subsidized bus passes. In the last decade an increasing percent of tertiary students have paid fees. In 1999/2000 private fees totaled about 12 percent of public expenditures for higher education.

Although the pre-tertiary level does not seem to have informal (unofficial) payments, an unknown amount of bribery of university faculty is reported to occur. The system has also arrears equivalent to 4.3 percent of the 1999 executed, unconsolidated central budget for education. There are no trend data on arrears by any level of education. Thus, what is perhaps the most critical question is whether the system is gradually reducing or increasing the stock of arrears. However, this cannot be evaluated. If data existed that showed that arrears were gradually being cleared and not augmented, the conclusion would be that the system is now on a sustainable footing, assuming that current levels of private financing continue.

Efficiency. Except for the tertiary level, declining student/teacher ratios indicate that labor is being used less efficiently, especially at the secondary level. Ratios of teaching to non-teaching staff for primary, secondary, and tertiary education are efficient relative to OECD standards. Annual teaching loads are efficient as well. Salaries for the education sector are below the average public sector wage, although differences in annual workloads between teachers and the average public sector employee, makes direct comparison difficult. Student/class unit ratios indicate that Croatia uses its classrooms intensively. Student/school ratios do not reveal large numbers of inefficient small schools. The fact that about 75 percent of schools are double shift and 7 percent are triple shift indicates an intensive use of schools. Higher education has serious internal efficiency problems. It is estimated that only a third of those enrolled complete. Of those that do complete, those in four-year degree programs take an average of seven years to complete; those in two-year programs, an average of five years to complete.

Equity. Poverty in Croatia is already strongly related to lower levels of education. As Croatia increasingly integrates into the global economy, human capital will increasingly affect Croats' employment probabilities, wages, and probabilities of being poor. Trends in gross enrollment rates are a country's human capital early warning system. However, unreliable population numbers make it difficult to track these rates.

In 1993-94 Croatia reformed secondary technical or vocational programs (VET-Vocational Education Training) reducing the academic requirements and creating three-year as well as four-year year options. A third of all secondary enrollments and 44 percent of those enrolled in VET are enrolled in the three-year programs that preclude access to university. In terms of creating the human capital needed in a modern economy, this reform was biased against the poor. In fact, students from poorer families are more apt to enroll in VET and more apt to enroll in the three-year vocational programs than in the four-year technical programs. Not only do the three-year programs preclude access to university, but they also have weak academic content and represent fewer years of total education for those that complete these programs.

The results for the tertiary level are consistent with higher education public policy. Although Government subsidizes accommodations and food for tertiary-level students from poor families, students with the highest secondary school grades and university entrance examination scores get their tuition publicly financed. Students from poor families are less apt to have high grades or scores and more apt to have to pay fees. The new draft Bill on Institutions of Higher Education proposes that all students pay tuition and that a student loan scheme be introduced to help families finance these costs. However, the poor are more reluctant to borrow. Public financing of higher education should include scholarships awarded on the basis of a combination of merit and family need.

Quality. Croatia has no interpretable evidence on the learning of its students. It does not know how they perform relative to Croatia-specific learning standards or relative to students from countries that will increasingly become Croatia's economic competitors and partners. However, indirect evidence suggests that Croatian students and young people would not perform well on an international assessment of information-processing skills needed in the workplace, home, and community.[62] The amount of time students spends in learning—"time on task"— affects the skills and knowledge acquired. The average Croatian child can expect to complete fewer years of education than OECD counterparts, and mandatory instructional time per year is lower in Croatia than for OECD countries, the gap being greatest at grades 1-4. The number of years of education of teachers is relatively low, as almost half of pre-tertiary educators (48.9 percent) do not have a four-year university degree.

Recommendations

General

- To expand private provision, clarify and simplify the processes and standards that private providers have to meet.

- As soon as the new census data are available, recalculate gross enrollment rates for all levels of education.

- Set and measure learning performance standards by grade and subject.

- Participate in international learning assessments to benchmark the performance of Croatia's education system against those of future competitors and partners. Use the results to assess "quality" and to identify policies that should increase quality.

Preschool education

- In consultation with local government officials and preschool educators, review preschool input norms for inefficiencies.

---

[62] Slovenian students' performance on an international quality assessment was relatively poor compared to students from other regional countries such as Czech Republic and Poland. Given the similarities of the Croatian and Slovenian education systems, one would expect similar performance of their students.

Primary education

- Eliminate all triple shift primary schools.

Secondary education

- Increase student/teacher ratios;

- Evaluate the adequacy of budgeting norms for non-staff recurrent expenses and increase resources for non-staff recurrent expenses (O&M);

- Increase completion rates for secondary education;

- Eliminate three-year VET secondary programs and increase the academic content of four-year VET programs;

University education

- Replace faculty-specific entrance examinations with nationally administered and graded examinations;

- Implement articles of the proposed Bill on Institutions of Higher Education that target incentives for students to complete programs quickly;

Targeted Cash-Transfer Programs: Social Assistance and Child Allowances

Social assistance in Croatia is characterized by poor coordination among the different programs, different eligibility criteria, and program rules that are often unclear to the beneficiaries. In addition, the implementation of these eligibility criteria is sometimes subject to the discretion of local officials. The system also allows for the possibility to collect benefits from multiple sources.[63] Therefore, in the current context, it is possible to achieve more substantial poverty reduction by reallocating funds and improving coordination among existing social programs. The following paragraphs will analyze two of the most important social programs: social assistance and child allowances. The analysis is not comprehensive and only intends to show the current type of problems existing within the social assistance sphere, and the range of possible policy actions.

Both the social assistance program and the child allowances program are targeted programs, though in different ways, and with somewhat different objectives. Traditionally, child allowances were intended for low-income workers, to ease some of the cost of child rearing and to minimize work disincentives at the lower end of the wage scale. In contrast, the primary focus of social welfare/social help programs of different types (cash and kind) was to deliver social services, cash and in-kind support to those unable to care for themselves, such as the disabled,

---

[63] Individuals can benefit from different income census applied by municipalities as oppose to thresholds applied by the centers for social care.

and elderly without support. This inheritance is important, as it remains relevant to current program objectives, and issues of stigma attached to programs.

Total spending in 1999 on what is now called the "support allowance" was around 290 million HRK, or 0.2 percent of GDP, paid to some 82,000 beneficiaries. This compared with around 1.1 billion HRK, or 0.77 percent of GDP, spent in the same year on child allowances paid to some 200 thousands households. Given the relative balance between the two programs, and the fact that they now essentially compete for the same limited general revenues, it is important to compare the extent to which they meet poverty reduction objectives. Analysis of 1998 HBS data reveals that the poverty reduction impact of one HRK allocated to social assistance is substantially greater than for the child allowance; nevertheless there was almost four times more spent on child allowances in that year than on social assistance. Despite differences in budgetary allocation to each of the two programs, the poverty headcount in Croatia would have been around 1.2 percentage points higher without social assistance spending,[64] but only 0.8 percentage points higher without child allowances. Given the relative spending patterns, this suggests a significantly more efficient use of resources within social assistance in terms of poverty reduction. This pattern is different to some neighboring countries such as Hungary, where family allowances outperform social assistance in poverty reduction terms.

Looking forward, the relative effectiveness of these two programs on poverty reduction becomes even more relevant in light of recent significant changes in child allowances, which entered into force in November 2000. These affect both eligibility and levels of benefit. On eligibility, coverage was widened to include all unemployed parents, and craftsmen and farmer households with children. This is a significant broadening from the previous coverage of only the employed in the legal entity sector, and the number of children covered by the program increased from around 380,000 (in around 200,000 households) in mid-2000 to around 600,000 (in around 400,000 households) in 2001. On the benefit side, a more complex two-income threshold system has been introduced, according to which benefits vary. Many of the previous additional entitlements for specific groups remain (e.g., single parents; those with handicapped children), including entitlement for defenders' families and refugees regardless of household income. Overall, the range of child allowance levels increased from between 123 HRK-331 HRK per month, to 166 HRK-375 HRK per month.

The rather complex eligibility and entitlement structure makes a robust estimate of additional fiscal costs difficult, but a simple adjustment according to increased beneficiaries would suggest that child allowance spending might increase by around 55 percent at a minimum, even making no allowance for increased benefit levels. This would add around 0.6 percent of GDP to social transfer spending on 2001. Assuming such a crude estimate gives a reasonable order of magnitude, this raises concerns about the additional call on budgetary revenues at a time when the budget deficit is already large, and there are extraordinary demands from pension restitution payments and other spending needs. There is, however, some flexibility under the new Law, which gives the Government the right to adjust eligibility thresholds in light of available funds in the budget. It is likely that real downward adjustment in eligibility thresholds will be needed, given the substantial increase in coverage.

---

[64] When including all cash assistance allowances, including payments outside the support allowance (equivalent to 0.54 percent of GDP in 1999).

Given the proposed changes in coverage, one would expect the poverty focus of child allowances to increase. Unemployed parents as a group have been found to be significantly poorer than average, with households with unemployed or inactive heads three times more likely than average to live in poverty. Equally, other correlates of poverty suggest that the inclusion of farmer/craftsmen households would be likely to improve the targeting of child allowances. In particular, household heads with low education are about twice as likely to be poor, a factor which is likely to be more prevalent in rural areas. While it is difficult to quantify such effects, if one considers the child allowance program in isolation, the recent reforms are likely to increase the targeting efficiency of the program.

However, the broader question in terms of poverty reduction impact of social transfers is whether increasing resources for child allowances is the most effective use of limited revenues, given the opportunity cost for other programs. This can only be assessed in light of the poverty profile. While the recent reforms are likely to improve the targeting of child allowances, they obviously continue to exclude households without children, and therefore imply a strong policy bias against households without children. In pure poverty terms, this is not justified by the poverty profile in 1998, where children had an about average poverty risk, while the elderly faced a higher than average poverty risk. Among the elderly, poverty was particularly severe among those without pensions and among those over 70 (the least likely to have remaining children in the household). Elderly without a pension are more than twice as likely to be poor, and have only social assistance/social welfare programs as their source of transfer income. The use of any additional transfer revenue in a way that has no impact on these groups is therefore a cause for concern.

Of course, there may well be objectives in social transfer policy other than poverty alleviation, and child allowances still retain the additional goals of minimizing disincentives for parents to work or re-enter work among the labor force, and to a limited extent smoothing income during child rearing years. Without empirical evidence as the new programs are implemented, it is difficult to make strong policy recommendations. However, from a poverty reduction viewpoint, social assistance is currently a better-targeted use of public resources on poverty reduction, and is likely to remain so even after the reforms of child allowance become effective. Given the additional fiscal pressure from child allowances in 2001, it will be critical to resist possible pressures to cut budgetary allocations to social assistance. The case for resisting such cuts is overwhelming when one considers other far less targeted spending within the safety net, most notably on veterans' programs.

Recommendations

- Increases in child allowance spending should not be at the expense of social assistance payments, as the latter are better targeted and already have very limited funding;

- Child allowance spending on 2001 will have to be closely monitored and reviewed on at least a quarterly basis, with adjustments made in the eligibility thresholds if the fiscal pressures of increased coverage are significant;

- It would be advisable to reconsider the automatic eligibility for child allowances of specific groups such as defenders' families if there is not solid evidence of them being categorically poorer than average;

- After a reasonable period (but probably no more than 12 months), the coverage and incidence of child allowances, as well as its poverty alleviation impact weighed relative to that of social assistance should be closely reviewed. Their relative funding should be reallocated accordingly;

- Determine the official poverty line and set eligibility criteria both at the CG as well as at the level of the local governments based on this line;

- Assess targeting effectiveness of different types of social assistance programs and reallocate funds accordingly.

Transport

Overview and issues. Transport in Croatia plays an important role not only in international trade, but also in reestablishing profitable transit traffic, promoting tourism and, ultimately, in unifying the country. Croatia has achieved a great deal in the transport sector in the short time since independence, repairing most war damage, writing laws which are generally suitable to govern the transport sector of a sovereign state, and privatizing some transport enterprises. However, the State still dominates the transport sector to an excessive degree;[65] the efficiency of most Croatian transport organizations is low; overall public sector spending in transport is high compared to other regional countries; and new investment projects in motorways are given too much emphasis at the expense of maintenance of the relatively abundant existing capacity.

Unconsolidated public transport expenditures of CGG and repayment of loans are more than 6 percent of GDP, which is relatively high by international standards. Moreover, under the previous government, Croatia initiated an ambitious program of motorway and other transport investments aimed at "catching up" with Western Europe, much of which appears uneconomic. In general, there is ample transport capacity in the country. However, much infrastructure is in fair or poor condition as maintenance was systematically deferred. Croatia needs to prioritize its investments carefully on the basis of economic criteria.

Croatia aspires to join the European Union (EU) where transport is overwhelmingly market oriented. However, the efficiency of most Croatian transport organizations leaves a lot to be desired. There is significant scope for further privatization and commercialization within the sector, as well as for reorienting the Government's direct management of the transport sector. This will also help to prepare transport enterprises to compete in the EU and to reduce total public transport expenditures in the medium term to around 3 percent of GDP, closer to the norm

---

[65] The exception being inter-city road transport.

for middle income countries. Specific recommendations for achieving these objectives are highlighted below.[66]

Expenditures and financing. Transport infrastructure and services are mostly financed through budgetary transfers, which have increased steadily from US$588 million equivalent in 1997 to US$768 million equivalent in 1999, with US$570 million budgeted in 2000. These expenditures include investments, maintenance, wages and operating costs, subsidies and other expenditures. In 1999, government transport expenditures included US$390 million for the local part of investments, US$112 million for maintenance, and US$233 million for subsidies. Additional transport expenditures also need to be taken into account:

- *Foreign financed investments/debt service.* The above budgetary expenditures do not include the foreign part of investments, nor the debt service on foreign transport loans paid directly by the Government. While separate figures are not available, these are likely to be of the order of US$100 million p.a.

- *Guarantees.* The Government paid out about US$125 million equivalent against transport guarantees in 1998. Guarantees contribute to distort the market by artificially improving the financial stance and competitiveness of the beneficiary companies. This practice should be discontinued. Guarantees given to public firms that compete with the private sector have a similar effect, as do operating subsidies (US$262 million proposed for 2001). In addition to these registered guarantees, there are hidden guarantees under the form of concession agreement provisions covering risks that normally should be borne by concessionaire, such as minimum revenue guarantees. While the Government should honor existing contracts, the issuance of new guarantees should be sharply curtailed.

- *Other transport expenditures.* These include the transport budgets of regional administrations and urban areas. While figures are not available, these are likely to be of the order of US$30 million p.a.

Public transport expenditures appear to have peaked at more than US$1 billion in 1999, or almost 6 percent of GDP. This is high compared to other countries. For example, the overall level of public expenditure on transport (excluding debt service and other financial costs) has been brought down to about 1-1.5 percent of GDP in Poland, which is similar to the level in the U.K. and France.

The previous Government prepared a *Transport Sector Policy Paper* (TSPP) which was approved in November 1999. The TSPP proposed a massive transport investment program of about US$ 20 billion equivalent during 2001-2010, or 5 percent of forecasted GDP p.a. This proposal included, among other things road maintenance expenditures, but did not include other operating and maintenance expenditures, LG expenditures, subsidies or guarantee repayments. The economic justification of most of the proposed investments is highly doubtful given the ample capacity of the existing system. Investment decisions should be driven by economic

---

[66] Further analysis is also provided in the World Bank report *Republic of Croatia: Policy Directions for Transport* dated June 15, 1999 (Report No. 19447-HR).

criteria if Croatia wants to avoid the pitfalls that bedeviled centrally planned economies in the past, and more recently, a number of East Asian economies. In the case of publicly owned infrastructure (roads, ports, railways), it is the role of the State to make investment decisions and be responsible for the consequences. It would be naïve, for example, to expect private investors to carry the commercial risk for a motorway project that is not financially viable. Other investment decisions, mainly for transport vehicles and equipment, such as trucks, ships, locomotives, or aircraft, should be driven by the commercial decisions of corporate managers operating in a competitive market. Extraneous considerations, such as the desire to have a large national airline, should not affect the decision making, as this would ultimately result in unprofitable enterprises that would pose a drain on budgetary resources. Transport investments are also not a good way to generate employment because they are capital intensive.

Most public expenditures should be devoted to maintaining and rehabilitating existing transport infrastructure, primarily highways, because these expenditures normally have a much higher priority and economic return than new transport investments. The maintenance of most transport infrastructure and equipment was deferred during and after the war due to budget constraints and the priority given to major new investments, primarily motorways. Only about 47 percent of national roads are in good condition, compared to 95 percent or more in most large West European countries. There are speed restrictions on 30 percent of railway lines, signaling and telecommunications systems are old to the point of obsolescence, and locomotive availability is a very low (55-65 percent), all due to deferred maintenance.

Efficiency. The efficiency of most transport operations is low resulting in high transport costs and a poor quality of service. For example, railway operating costs are a high US$0.15 per traffic unit (tkm+pkm) due to low productivity. Hrvatske Zeljeznice (HZ; Croatian Railways) staff productivity was 143,000 traffic units per employee in 1999, about half the level observed in Slovenia or the Czech Republic and one-quarter the level observed in Poland and Germany. HZ also requires an unnecessarily large fleet of traction and rolling stock to offset its poor condition. The cost of transit through the Port of Rijeka (port dues and cargo handling charges per ton) appears to be about twice the level of North Sea ports (Rotterdam, Hamburg), while labor productivity is only about one-eighth that of efficient Mediterranean ports (Marseilles, Israeli ports). There is a worldwide recession in shipping and shipbuilding, and it appears that Croatian shipping is inefficiently utilized, which has prompt Government's direct as well as indirect subsidies. Public for-hire trucks travel an inefficiently low 39,000-km/vehicle/annum and own-account trucks an even lower 25,000 km/vehicle/annum. It is estimated that road vehicle operating costs and road maintenance/rehabilitation costs are about 10 percent higher than necessary due to inadequate maintenance funding as discussed below.

Scope for private sector intervention. There is now an over-whelming majority opinion in the EU, other countries and academia, that the private sector runs transport operations much more efficiently than the State. Transport companies will be exposed to a significantly higher level of competition in the EU, and it is important to increase efficiency to prepare for possible accession. A five-year privatization action plan could include the following steps:

- The privatization of inter-city road transport of passengers and freight should be completed. At the same time, State-owned enterprises should rapidly phase out their own-account transport services that are generally inefficient and expensive.

Selective privatization of urban transport services has been done in some countries with good results, but needs careful preparation and regulation.

- The outright sale of a majority of equity, including to strategic investors, should be envisaged for Jadrolinija and other shipping lines, shipbuilding enterprises, river transport operators and Croatia Airlines. In parallel, these markets should be opened to competition for both national and international services, with a view to reap the economic benefits and efficiency gains that are associated with competitive markets.

- Port operations at Rijeka and Ploce should be privatized.

- As regards railways, there is now a large body of experience demonstrating that railways can be successfully privatized. Outright sale of assets has been the method of choice in the U.S., Japan and Great Britain. It has been very successful in the U.S. and Japan. Concessions of various forms have been awarded mainly in a number of Latin American countries and have been also very successful. Restructuring initiatives are also getting underway in Central Europe, e.g., Poland, Slovenia and Romania. The 1994 Law on Croatian Railways as well as the recently adopted Strategy for HZ restructuring includes the privatization of subsidiaries and the creation of a joint stock company, but much more needs to be done.

In a market economy, transport is primarily performed by private organizations, while specific social services are compensated by public service obligations (PSOs). The role of the Ministry of Maritime Affairs, Transport, and Communications (MMATC) should thus be reoriented from its former role of directly managing transport enterprises, to a market-oriented role where the main tasks are to assure that competition among private transport operators is fair, and to protect the public interest in safety, the environment and social working conditions.

Since independence, Croatia has adopted numerous transport laws intended to move Croatia toward a market economy transport system also consistent with EU practices. It will require a major effort to implement these laws, monitor results and make modifications where required, as well as monitor the development of the EU regulatory framework and the experience of the pre-accession countries. It is recommended that this task be centralized in MMATC, which should also monitor the performance, planning and budgeting of the transport system. The MMATC will require institutional strengthening to take on these responsibilities. As a practical matter, MMATC may wish to delegate some of these responsibilities to Croatian Roads (HC), HZ and other transport operators.

Recommendations

- Define and implement a program to reduce the role of Government in the transport sector and privatize transport operations.

- Carry out cost/benefit assessments, as a part of the budgetary process, based on realistic traffic forecasts for all proposed major public transport investments, including rehabilitation/replacement projects, and rank public investments in order of economic priority, deferring those with economic rates of return less than 12 percent until traffic develops.

- Estimate the likely future cost of guarantees and other contingent liabilities (e.g., revenue guarantees) using actuarial techniques and include this provision in the 2002 budget; minimize the use of guarantees and other extra-budgetary obligations in the future.

- Provide operating subsidies only where it is desired to subsidize a transport service on social grounds, e.g., suburban passenger services, inter island ferries. The subsidy should be designated as a PSO payment for the specific service, and preferably paid by the concerned regional or local government.

If these recommendations are followed, it should be possible to bring total unconsolidated public transport expenditures down to 3 percent of GDP (less than 2 percent of GDP on a consolidated basis) while at the same time increasing its efficiency in preparation for increasing cooperation with the EU.

Defense

The Government of Croatia plans to continue with the reduction of expenditure that has characterized the sector over the course of the past five years. Croatia's spending on defense stands at 2.9 percent of GDP[67] (2000) down from 9.4 percent of GDP at its peak in 1995. Adjustment to the new peace conditions allowed this important reduction in defense expenditures in only five years (1995-2000). Nevertheless, if the Government wants to align its defense expenditures to European standards

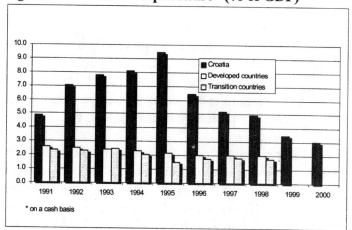

Figure 2.12: Defense Expenditure* (% of GDP)

* on a cash basis

Source: Ministry of Finance and World Bank estimates.

it will have to impose further cuts in the sector in the order of 0.8 percent of GDP. However, if the Government wants also to align the internal costs structure of the sector with that in the rest of Europe, it will have to concentrate the bulk of the reductions in reducing personnel costs.

Expenditure in defense has experienced substantial changes over the past 10 years. Recorded sector spending almost doubled its allocation as a share of GDP, going from less than 5 percent in 1991 to 9.4 percent in 1995, the year of the last war episode. However, actual spending on defense is believed to have reached much higher levels during the war years, as some defense spending was hidden behind a deliberately obscure budget management process used during the early independence years; while some defense spending was financed from

---

[67] On accrual basis.

sources outside the budget. In fact, anecdotal evidence points to the use of privatization receipts never accounted for within the budget to finance the war effort. These, as well as the use of foreign exchange accounts held abroad could have been used by the previous government to circumvent the budget in the purchase of defense equipment.

From 1995 onwards, the defense budget contracted by almost 6.5 percent of GDP. Although part of this reduction is the mere result of changes in accounting practices,[68] most of it is genuine, being the result of the demobilization process that occurred after the last military action in 1995. However, as stated in the government financial reports, this reduction was based on a contraction of non-wage recurrent expenditures. In fact, government financial reports show a contraction in the defense wage bill, including employers' contributions, of about 19 percent of GDP from 1995 to 2000; while non-wage current defense spending shrank by approximately 4.9 percent of GDP. Even though we had no access to the number of demobilized personnel, the reduction of non-wage recurrent expenditures is believed to be at least partially linked to the reduction of non-regular military personnel, the majority of whom were 'contracted out'. As such, these non-regular military personnel were not within the payroll of the Ministry of Defense. They were allegedly paid through cash compensations and consequently recorded as non-wage spending.

Figure 2.13: Structure of Defense

Figure 2.14: Adjustment of Defense Sector to Peace Time

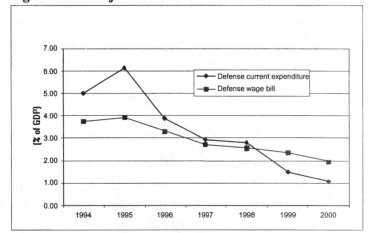

Source: Ministry of Finance and World Bank.

---

[68] Up until 1999, some non-defense expenditure, such as budget transfers to Bosnia and Herzegovina (equivalent to 0.4 percent of GDP in 1999), were hidden under the defense budget and are now properly accounted for as international transfers, under the MoF's budget. Similarly, some capital transfers to the Ministry of Defense used for building civilian roads by engineering ground troops, previously recorded as defense spending are, since 1999, accounted for as capital transfers for roads reconstruction (equivalent to 0.2 percent of GDP in 1999).

Consequently, the reduction of these non-regular personnel would, in turn, help explain the big contraction of non-wage current defense expenses.[69]

Although there is no reliable data available on total employment in the defense sector, Central Bureau of Statistics estimates point to some 72,000 employees in defense and police. This is around 5.5 percent of total official employment in Croatia. The new Government has already introduced important cuts in defense and plans to continue reducing expenses in this area as well as in police spending, mainly by reducing the number of army and police personnel. Currently, almost 70 percent of spending in defense is allocated to wages and related compensations, while only 30 percent is spent on the modernization of defense equipment. This is not in line with defense spending patterns in NATO member countries. In fact, NATO standard requires much higher spending on equipment, while wages represent less than 40 percent of total defense spending. Giving the existing structure of expenditure, heavily biased towards wages and allowances, one could expect further personnel retrenchment, especially in ground troops and the ministry itself.

In reshaping the labor force of the defense sector, particular attention should be devoted to the employees of the ministry itself. The educational structure of the administrative component of the sector (the personnel of the ministry) is significantly below the average for the CG. Compared to the average for the CG where 53 percent of employees hold secondary and non-university degrees and 32 percent hold university degrees, the educational attainment profile of those employed in defense is much more concentrated towards secondary and primary education levels (50 and 42 percent of total defense employment, respectively).[70] This, in turn, makes the potential redundant employees less re-employable, making their lay-offs relatively more costly and politically less acceptable. To avoid adverse selection problems at the time of retrenchment, and to retain the better qualified employees, the retrenchment process should be carefully designed, including the identification of redundant employees, when possible, and the crafting of severance packages that would contribute to the release of less qualified personnel, when direct identification is not possible.

If the realignment of defense expenditure to Western-European standards were to be carried out solely by cutting down on wage spending on the sector, this would require some 16,000 to 20,000 lay-offs in the sector. This would be an upper bound estimation as not all the adjustment is expected to come from cuts in personnel. Nevertheless, in order to assess the costs and savings associated with this reduction one can assume two extreme scenarios. In the first scenario, everyone of those declared redundant will get a one-time severance package in the amount of approximately US$5,000 per person[71] and will then get the highest available unemployment benefit until they find a job, with none of them going into retirement. In the second scenario, 50 percent of laid-off employees would go into retirement as war veterans while

---

[69] Part of the 'peace dividend' generated by the lower defense spending, was "consumed" by the expansion in social spending related to the demobilization of soldiers, as many of those leaving the army went into early retirement or qualified for unemployment benefits.

[70] The analysis was done based on a sample of employees of the Ministry itself, which, if anything, could be upward biased in terms of the educational achievement of the defense personnel.

[71] In accordance with current laws regulating obligatory severance payment, US$5,000 is the result of multiplying the average wage in the sector by the estimated average working years in the army (currently around five).

the other 50 percent would go through early retirement as Croatian army. The results of these two scenarios are shown below:

Table 2.6: Annual Social Costs for Defense Employment Reduction (% of GDP)

Scenario 1: no pension, severance package and unemployment benefit		Scenario 2: 50% war veterans' and 50% Croatian army pension	
1st year	2nd year and until new employment	1st year	2nd year and after
0.46-0.57%	0.10-0.13%	0.47-0.59%	0.47-0.59%

Source: Staff Calculations.

Starting in 1999, a more transparent presentation of the defense budget has facilitated a more thorough discussion of defense issues, inside and outside Parliament, inducing the Government to implement a further rationalization of defense spending and introduce better budget management. Defense expenditure remains at some 0.8 percent of GDP above the average for European economies, after five years since the last war episode and yet, the defense sector is responsible for a stock of arrears amounting to 0.65 percent of GDP (1999). If Croatia is to align its level of expenditure on defense with that in other European countries, it will be able to achieve additional annual savings of close to 1.0 percent of GDP. However, the minimum social costs related to lay-offs will partially offset the savings by 0.46-0.57 percent of GDP in the year of adjustment. These costs would fall in subsequent years, in an amount that would depend on the option chosen with costs ranging from 0.1 to 0.6 percent of GDP in the next few years.

Recommendations

- If the Government wants to realign defense expenditure levels and the internal cost structure to Western-European standards, then the bulk of the reductions should be aimed at reducing personnel;

- To avoid adverse selection problems at the time of retrenchment the retrenchment should be carefully designed, including the identification of redundant employees, when possible, and the crafting of severance packages that would contribute to the release of less qualified personnel, when direct identification is not possible;

- Attention should be paid to indirect fiscal costs of retrenchment, in the form of pensions and severance payments;

- Granting of early retirement special concessions should be ruled out;

- The sector should also identified and divest unnecessary real state property and other non-core assets owned by the army and the Ministry of Defense, reducing maintenance and administration costs.

LATEST DEVELOPMENTS

While this Report was being finalized, the Government started to implement a new wave of measures, most of which are contained in this Report and were discussed with the Government at the time of this Report's dissemination. The changes include both reforms to public sector expenditure allocation and changes to budgetary processes. Regarding the restructuring of public spending for fiscal retrenchment, the Government, in 2001, introduced dramatic changes in the compensation schemes for public sector employees. Trying to reduce the 2001 CCG wage bill by some 9 percent in nominal terms, the Government restructured the system of job grade coefficients to harmonize salary payment across ministries making use of a new government employees' law. This reform also aimed at reducing the overall wage bill. In this regard, the Government initiated a reduction in the public sector workforce, by eliminating some 1,500 employees from the payroll of the ministry of Interior by mid-year, and leaving their future working engagement with the public sector to the decision of the Government. Further personnel reductions currently in preparation, are planned to push net employment reductions to 10,000 employees in 2001, almost 70 percent of which would come from the Ministry of Defense following the upcoming approval of a new Defense law. Personnel reductions will be carried out under less generous severance payments, the result, in turn, of the aforementioned public employee's law. In addition, the Government eliminated the meal allowance from the gross wage and reduced the required notice period for dismissal from 3-36 months to 6 months, while Government officials' wages were lowered by 7 percent.

Social transfer are to be substantially revised. A package of ten laws is already in the Parliament; this package would set the legal basis to, among other things, decrease the replacement rate for sick pay leave while shortening the maximum period of sick leave before facing an assessment commission to six months; and shorten the maternity leave to no more than one year per child. Regarding the child benefit program, the package is aimed at reducing the duration of the allowance, reducing the range of beneficiaries exempted from mean-testing, and setting a cap on the family-wide allowance. In addition, privileged pensions were decreased by 8-20 percent while a cap on these pensions was established. The measures would include also a cap on overall social assistance benefits. In the area of health, co-payments for hospital services, drugs and other health services are expected to be raised, the categories of exempted beneficiaries reduced, and the range of services subject to co-payment broadened. On the revenues side, beside the aforementioned measures on co-payments for health, the new veterans' law proposal would eliminate payroll tax exemptions for defenders, invalids and survivors' pensions.

CHAPTER 3: IMPROVING BUDGETARY MANAGEMENT

INTRODUCTION AND OVERVIEW

Chapter 2 examined a number of allocative and efficiency issues that demand attention as the Government rationalizes the role of the public sector in the economy. While this external overview provides some clear indications of areas where a reorientation and restructuring of expenditures is required, it does not provide a complete analysis of expenditure issues in Croatia nor can it substitute for a political process that determines strategic priorities for the Government. Therefore, a crucial element of public sector reform is a reform of budgetary management practices to ensure that institutional arrangements and processes are put in place that allow policy makers to make strategic policy choices based on an informed analysis of public expenditure issues, to transform those choices into actions, to ensure budget expenditures are monitored and audited, and to make budgetary choices and outcomes transparent to all elements of society.

This Chapter, therefore, focuses on Croatia's system of fiscal management and the primary institutions involved in the process. It also examines the operation of the budget system, how decisions are made, and how the key institutions fulfill their assigned roles.

Croatia has already made significant progress in improving public expenditure management in the past decade. Key reforms that have been made are:

- Passage of a new budget law in 1994;

- Movement toward a Consolidated Treasury Fund;

- Efforts in privatization and financial system restructuring;

- Establishment of an external audit body in 1993;

- Reform of the Social Accounting Office (early 1990's); and

- Introduction of a Three-year Rolling Public Investment Program in 1996.

These developments are all the more impressive when one realizes that they occurred against a backdrop of transitioning to a market economy, establishing an independent nation, enduring an armed conflict and subsequently, restructuring a war-torn economy.

As a result of these reforms, the existing fiscal management system can be described as follows. The national budget and accounting system are cash-based while the financial management system largely rests on the hands of the ministries. The main processes are:

- *Budget formulation*. Primary role of formulating budgets, planning, and improving the efficiency and effectiveness of public spending is decentralized to each Ministry;

- *Budget execution and cash management.* Budget execution is centralized in the MoF, but cash management is undertaken through accounts maintained by each Ministry. Cash management is being centralized into a Treasury Consolidated Fund (single treasury account); and

- *Internal control and auditing.* Responsibility for internal control and auditing is assigned to each Ministry.

Although it is standard practice for line Ministries to take the lead in policy and planning for their sector; there is a role at the center for the MoF in setting standards, coordinating government-wide financial issues, analyzing policy issues and budget developments, and supporting central decision-making bodies (e.g., Cabinet). In Croatia, these central MoF functions are not well developed. The MoF has limited capacity to develop budget options, push public finance reforms, monitor and control spending, and enforce current laws and regulations.

Assignment of policy development functions to line ministries within the CG without adequate development of the central financial management functions allows non-standard methods to be employed, results in varying degrees of quality in spending unit data and procedures, and generates uncertainty regarding spending, accounting, and program results. As a consequence, the current public finance system in Croatia has very limited mechanisms for accountability, whether over finances, policy, or actual spending program results.

In light of the aforementioned characteristics of the budget process in Croatia, key elements of a strategy to improve budget performance would include:

- Strengthening the central organizations overseeing budgeting, treasury functions, and internal control;

- Developing standardized accounts, budgets, and procedures for public financial management;

- Strengthening enforcement mechanisms through improved internal control and auditing; and

- Moving all revenues and spending on budget to allow managing of public finances at a national level.

The rest of this Chapter is organized as follows: Section B discusses general budget issues, including the comprehensiveness of the current budget, and the outcome of the budget control process. Section C reviews the current process of budget formulation. Section D discusses budget execution, internal auditing, addresses the level of control in budget execution rather than the process itself, as well as the current internal control structure. Section E briefly considers the current role of Parliament, the State Audit Office, and the Supreme Audit Institution. Section F provides a general assessment of the current Budget Law, with particular emphasis on current financial management practices and how these could be strengthened through changes to the Law. Each section includes a series of recommendations for strengthening public expenditure management in the Republic of Croatia. The recommendations are then summarized in Annex C. Finally, since the discussion of this Report with the Government, a number of actions have been taken or are planned. These measures are briefly discussed in Section G.

GENERAL BUDGET ISSUES

Before analyzing budgetary management processes, it is essential to examine the scope of the budget to ensure that it is a comprehensive measure of fiscal activity in the country. The analysis undertaken in this report, in close collaboration with USAID, indicates that the current budget in Croatia is not comprehensive in four key aspects:

- Five extra-budgetary funds are not included in the budget;

- Off-budget revenues, outside of the extra-budgetary funds, still exist;

- The cash budgeting system leads to the accumulation of arrears that do not appear in budget presentations;

- Laws enacted outside of the budget process lead to overspending.

The current budget of the Republic of Croatia does not include all national spending as five extra-budgetary funds (EBFs) allocate more than 50 percent of the CCG total spending. Maintaining these EBFs as such (off-budget) is misleading with respect to the financial condition of the CG. The deficit of the EBFs widened from 6.1 percent of GDP in 1997 to 10.2 in 1999, falling to 8.5 percent of GDP in 2000, most of which was financed by transfers from the Budget and to a lesser extent, by accumulation of arrears. Off-budget accounting does not shield the Government from these liabilities. The CHII alone accumulated HRK 3.5 billion in arrears up to 1999. Moreover, the earmarked revenues for two EBFs (Children's and Water Management Fund) have been abolished since July 1, 1998; with expenditures directly supported from the Budget.

All public funds should be subject to the same regulations, controls, and standards of accountability; particularly, given the size of the EBFs, their recent growth, and the recent arrears accumulation. Within the budget, these activities can still be accounted for separately under Fund Accounting, but they would be subject to the same budget formulation and execution conditions as all other public funds.

Recommendations

- Amend the Budget Law to include all EBFs in the Budget.

- For the Children's and Water Management Fund, which no longer have earmarked revenue sources, consider making them programs within Ministries rather than separate funds.

Beyond the earmarked contributions for the EBFs, Ministries also receive off-budget revenues from fees, licenses, and other activities. Own revenues for 1999 are estimated at HRK 1.75 billion, or 3.8 percent of on-budget 1999 CG revenues, only HRK 80 million (4.5 percent of own revenues) of these revenues were included in the budget. Ministries are allowed to keep these 'own revenues' and use them as they choose.

The lack of transparency, which allows results from these revenues remaining off-budget, distorts resource allocation decisions of policymakers. It also prevents the Parliament and citizens from making informed decisions on government programs and activities. Finally, under the current Croatian cash budget there is a potential for commitments to be made from own revenues that exceed available revenues, which would fall against central budget funds.

Recommendation

- Bring all sources of revenue on-budget. Ministries can still be allowed to retain own-revenues for their use, but they must be included in budget submissions and subject to the same budget controls as other public funds.[72]

A basic test of any public finance system is the ability to control budget spending. Under a cash budget system, it can be misleading to look only at official deficits, as cash outlays can be 'controlled' by not paying obligations. Further, where internal controls and auditing are not well established, a spending unit may not enter the commitment into the accounting system until well after it is due. In Croatia, the significant, accumulation of arrears is a strong indication that budgets are not being controlled. In Ledger 2 of the 2000 Budget, the MoF identified HRK 9.5 billion in outstanding arrears.

An August 2000 USAID-financed report on liabilities indicates that roughly one-third of the accumulated arrears as of end-1999 arose from current spending.[73] Anecdotal evidence from interviews with budget execution staff at the MoF also indicate that they do receive requests for payment above budget (cash) allotments, when the goods or services have been received by Government and the Government already has a financial obligation to pay.

Moreover, some government spending is occurring "automatically," because some programs, such as health insurance, have eligibility and benefits determined in law. The Health Fund has no ability to change spending levels arising from these eligibilities and benefits. The Health Fund also does not determine the level of revenues to finance its activities. Where there is a structural imbalance between revenues and expenditures, over-commitment of funds occurs automatically.

---

[72] Not allowing Ministries to receive the benefit of revenues they collect will eliminate their incentive to generate and collect these revenues. Where the activities that generate revenues compete with the private sector or are subsidized from the central budget, it may be appropriate to attribute revenues to the central budget rather than to the Ministry.

[73] "Identification, Review and Analysis of Recorded and Unrecorded Liabilities," USAID Fiscal Reform Program, Prepared by Paul Stroh, KPMG Barents Group LLC, August 2000, p.5.

For on-budget spending, the current budget law does require the Government to submit legislative changes to achieve budgeted levels, as well as require Parliament to identify funding sources for any increase in spending or reduction in revenues. While these provisions are not always applied to on-budget spending, they do not apply to off-budget spending. Thus, if the Government lowers budget contributions to the Health Fund, the Fund automatically runs arrears, and the Government is under no requirement to balance the budget. Of course, the Government will have to directly address the arrears at some point, particularly when it begins to affect the provision of health services.

Recommendations

- Adopt modified accrual (commitment-based) budgeting, in which revenues are recognized when measurable and available, while expenditures are recognized when incurred (regardless of whether actually paid). This would require a change in the budget law.

- Adopt a policy of MoF review and approval of contracts prior to contract signature (Box 3.1).

Various techniques exist for funding programs. The most direct and transparent approach is simply to provide funds for a project or program directly in the annual budget bill. A second, less transparent approach to funding programs is mandatory spending. Mandatory spending encompasses laws, frequently passed outside the budget process, that require certain expenditures or transfers be made. Such laws may not appear to have a direct cost associated with them, as they seek only to 'reallocate' spending within current budget totals. But, they do have a cost, as they reduce budget transparency, avoid annual budget scrutiny, and limit the ability of governments to manage spending during budget execution.

One example of mandatory spending in the Croatian public finance system is Article 28 of the Law on War Veterans (*Official Gazette No. 108/96*), which requires 2 percent of every construction project funded with budget funds to be transferred to the Ministry of Public Works[74] for war veterans. While supporting war veterans may be a worthy cause; funds for this program should be directly provided in annual budgets if the Government and Parliament decide this particular program deserves support.

Funding a program through a non-transparent, mandatory transfer from other capital projects has several problems:

- It distorts the cost of other capital projects (where the budgeted cost is likely to rise by 2 percent to cover cost of the transfer).

- It creates uncertain funding for the war veterans programs as it is entirely dependent on how many capital projects are in the budget.

- It avoids annual decisions by Government and Parliament about what level of budget support to provide the veterans' program.

---

[74] Formerly, Ministry of Construction, Reconstruction, and Public Works.

- It funds non-capital programs with capital expenses, which can create a loophole through which borrowing is used to fund current budget expenses.

Box 3.1: Suggestions for Improved Commitment Control

- Spending Ministries must have a signature from the MoF certifying that funds are available, that the contract is within budget levels, and that the contract provisions comply with current financial and procurement requirements.

- Both Ministries and vendors must be made aware that unless the MoF has signed off on the contract in advance, the contract will not be considered valid, and expenditures against the contract will not be paid.

- Vendors must look for MoF approval on the contract before they can safely deliver goods and services and expect payment. Vendor cooperation is an essential element of commitment control, as it prevents delivery of goods and services in the absence of available funding. Some caution must be taken in implementing this in the Health Fund, as it may impact the delivery of medicines or other critical supplies.

- The MoF should establish a 'contract review task force', staffed by some 30 or more people to review contracts. The managers of the task force should be MoF personnel. However, the MoF could request that ministries provide people for the task force (under the condition that they will not review the contracts for their own ministries).

- MoF staff should draft a checklist for the use of reviewers of what contract provisions to look for, and who in the budget execution or consolidation offices to contact regarding fund availability.

- Set-up a spreadsheet or other mechanism for recording all contracts received and approved. This is the basis of a commitment monitoring and control system.

- To make the process more manageable, thresholds could be set for contract review (e.g., all contracts over Kuna 100,000 must be reviewed). Once the MoF feels it has a reasonable control over commitments, and other procedures are developed (SAP commitment module), then the contract review task force can be ended.

- Other commitments arise from hiring of personnel. The Budget Execution Office currently receives lists of employees from each Ministry prior to authorizing payroll. This must be scrutinized carefully to assure the current hiring freeze is enforced. It should be made explicit to Ministries that no paychecks will be issued for employees hired in contravention of the Government hiring freeze or in excess of budgeted levels.

Source: Staff

A more prevalent example of mandatory spending occurs in health insurance and health services. Health laws frequently define the health benefits and services that must be paid for by the insurance, and the population eligible to receive benefits. These two conditions effectively determine the expenditures of a health program. These expenditures, therefore, occur 'automatically' every year, with no government action required in annual budget laws. This situation can become problematic where the revenues are also fixed in annual budget laws, there is a 'structural imbalance' between revenues and expenses, and the agency charged with managing a health fund has no authority to control spending.

Social welfare benefits also fall into the category of mandatory spending, where the eligible population and benefit are defined in law. Funding for social welfare benefits usually remain in the annual budget, but obvious problems occur when annual budgets 'reduce' a budget allocation for social welfare benefits, when the underlying law still requires the same benefits be paid to the same population. Unless the underlying law is changed, arrears inevitably result.

Recommendations

- Identify those programs or activities in which actual spending is driven by laws outside the budget cycle.

- Identify all mandatory transfer of funds within the budget, such as the 2 percent transfer from capital projects to veterans programs.

- Convert the programs funded through these transfers away from mandatory transfers to direct budget support, unless there is a compelling rationale or public policy benefit.

GOVERNMENT BUDGET FORMULATION

The current Republic of Croatia Budget Law (*Official Gazette Number 92/94*) delineates the major steps in the formal budget process (Box 3.2).[75] As noted earlier, an important part of the Croatian budget formulation process is placed with line Ministries. The Government relies heavily on each line Ministry for assuring that sectoral policies are optimal, spending is efficient and effective, and programs operate under sound financial principles.

Box 3.2: Croatia: Budget Formulation Timeline	
July	MoF prepares economics and fiscal policy report for budget year, including guidelines and objectives of fiscal policy, and estimates for revenues and expenditures, and submits to the Government.
September	MoF issues guidance to spending Ministries on development of the budget, including procedures, expenditure targets, and deadlines. Guidance based on Government-approved fiscal policy report.
October 10	MoF transmits budget to Government for discussion.
November 15	Government sends budget to Parliament.

Source: Staff.

The budget formulation process starts in the MoF, when the macroeconomic forecasting unit develops forecasts for the economy and revenues. Based on these forecasts, the office responsible for budget formulation determines an overall expenditure envelope and allocates expenditure ceilings to each ministry. These estimates are primarily based on previous year allocations and may reflect some known government priorities. However, a key problem is the lack of integration of strategic priorities into budget allocations.

---

[75] Annex B presents a more detailed chronology of the current Croatian budget formulation process in the Government, including some of the types of information that flow between participants in the process.

These expenditure allocations, in the form of a call letter, are sent to the ministries. Ministries do not begin their budget development until the initial call memorandum is received from the MoF. Ministries are largely passive participants in the budget process.[76] In almost all cases, Ministries do not develop policies for various budget contingencies, identify options for reducing spending, nor prepare sound proposals for any new initiatives or programs prior to receiving the call letter.

Once the MoF call memorandum is received, Ministries begin preparing their budgets requests. These are usually prepared in two or three separate pieces, depending on the nature of the Ministry:

- Recurrent spending;

- Capital spending;

- Transfers.

Recurrent spending is prepared using traditional input-based methods, either taking the prior year level of activity multiplied by average cost (adjusted for inflation) to develop a 'current services' budget, or adjusting the current services for 'needed' level of activity. These estimates are prepared by program offices within each Ministry (or social organizations where actual services are delivered by third parties). Ministry budget offices perform minimal reviews of requests received, mainly reviewing for compliance with normative cost guidance.

Capital spending requests are prepared separately from recurrent spending. Ministry budget offices have separate capital investment units that prepare these materials. Ministries do try to prioritize projects, but do not perform detailed analysis of the cost of the project, appropriateness of the investment, etc. Again, the most analysis that is done by Ministry budget staff is whether project costs seem significantly out of line with past experience. Capital projects may be prioritized in terms of normatives (e.g., number of hospital beds per 1,000 population), but not in terms of a sectoral development strategy. Despite a MoF requirement to provide operating cost estimates for new capital spending, it is not clear these are used (in some cases, not even filled out), or incorporated into recurrent expenditure planning. Croatian budgets have traditionally looked only at one year, and not multi-year. The out-year effects of some capital spending are therefore not transparent to decision-makers.

Capital projects may also be partially funded in annual budgets. For example, a school construction project may receive in the current budget enough funding to start the project (e.g., 15 percent of project costs), with the assumption that remaining planned amounts will be funded annually until project completion. This approach permits the Government to fund a greater number of new projects per year, but may mean that this recurrent capital spending becomes a liability in future years (displacing new investments).

---

[76] In preparing this report, it was noted that the Ministry of Labor is beginning to develop a proactive policy development function. For the 2001 budget, the budget office prepared an options paper for the Minister for reducing costs and prioritizing spending.

Transfers are also not subjected to rigorous budget analysis or policy development by line Ministry budget offices. Line ministry budget offices pass the MoF budget call request on to the beneficiary of funds, asking for their proposed budget. Again, budget examination only occurs at the level of normative input costing. Absent any problems with costing, the line Ministry simply passes along the transfer budget request to the MoF.

Ministries generally submit their entire request (recurrent, capital, and transfers) to the MoF, with little regard for the spending target assigned to them in the guidance. Ministries felt that it was important to let the MoF know what they "really needed to fulfill their missions." Line Ministries usually do not include extensive budget justification materials, or even explanations of what the request would buy.

The MoF usually responds to ministry requests by reducing the request back to the target level, or lower if budget prospects have deteriorated. There is an absence of discussion or dialogue. The MoF does not probe in detail the ministry request or discuss policy. No guidance is given to line ministries regarding what areas to reduce spending for, or what programs they should not reduce. Line Ministries are left to their best professional judgment. This practice limits the ability of the MoF or the Cabinet to prevent line ministries from making untenable political choices. There is another problem that arises: mandatory and discretionary outlays are not clearly identified; this contributes to blur discussions on budget allocations.

This brief caricature of the budget formulation process in Croatia indicates that there is a need for a more robust budget process, with stronger accountability and more substantive dialogue. Areas for improvement include:

- The use of a multi-year budget framework;

- The use of objective analysis of policies, current spending, and policy options;

- Better data availability (chart of accounts);

- The provision of output data, and a focus on outputs;

- The strengthening of the interface between budget formulation and execution.

The current budget process in Croatia is notable for the lack of objective analysis and preparation of formal policy options for decision makers. Different types of analysis are necessary to support various types of decisions in a budget formulation process. Table 3.1 outlines the types of analysis that should be performed, and which organizations in government typically perform such analysis. Table 3.1 also outlines how these analyses are currently undertaken in the Croatian context. The types of analysis are broadly categorized by the level of aggregation of funds that are addressed: macroeconomic; public sector budget (the size of public resource consumption); sectoral or functional allocations (within public sector spending); organizational (translating sectoral or functional allocations to ministry allocations); and more traditional budget examination (reviewing spending by program and agency).

In formulating annual budgets, governments can be tempted to use overly optimistic forecasts of macroeconomic variables to inflate revenue forecasts and lessen the apparent need to reduce spending. These overly optimistic forecasts, on one hand, contribute to continued accumulation of arrears and shortage of cash. On the other hand, this can adversely affect external lenders' perceptions of economic management and performance. International financial markets quickly detect inflated economic forecasts, and the Government conveys the impression it is trying to avoid prudent fiscal management. These doubts can be translated into the country risk profile, raising premiums for foreign capital.[77] The use of modest forecasts yields the possibility that the economy will grow faster than forecasts, generating surplus revenues, which can be invested or used to pay down the debt. On the other hand, overly optimistic forecasts minimizes the potential for good news.

Table 3.1: Aggregations of Analysis in Budget Processes

'Best Practice' Budget Process			Current Practice in Croatia	
Type of Analysis	**Description**	**Responsible Organization**	**Responsible Organization**	**Analysis Performed**
Macro-economic	Estimates of the macro-environment, with particular attention to the interactive influences between Govt. revenues and spending and the economy.	MoF or MoE, Central Bank, professional staff of legislature, or all	MoE, MoF's Macroeconomic Unit	Yes. Forecast developed in MoF. MoE involved in developing government fiscal policy.
Public Sector Budget	Given the macroeconomic estimates, and economic policies, examination of the key government variables: tax rates (type and level); spending (level, current and capital); deficits and debt (level, policy towards, and financing); cash flow considerations.	MoF or MoE, professional staff of legislature	MoF	No. Spreadsheets are prepared estimating expend. and deficits, but no analysis on the appropriate size or role of Gov. is done, nor of the impact of policies on the economy, or constraints facing Govt. spending options.
Sectoral/ Functional	Examination of the major functions or sectors of Gov. spending (e.g., health, education, social welfare, defense, justice), including few sentinel indicators of national welfare for each function (e.g., life expectancy, educational attainment). Include international comparisons (regional averages as well as best and least comparisons). This can roughly indicate where further additional investments should be made, and from which sectors it can come. This analysis generally starts from the over-all policies set in preceding analysis, and focuses on how best to distribute revenues. Attention should also be paid to	MoF or MoE, and/or office of chief executive. Independent review may also be made by professional staff of legislative branch.	Spending Ministries	No. Current process assumes these analyses are performed at ministry level. However, ministries do not perform these analyses.

---

[77] A telling example for Croatia is Merrill Lynch's June 5, 2000, *Emerging Markets Daily* on Croatia, which observed that *"GDP fell in 1999 by 0.3 percent, whereas the 1999 budget was based on a growth assumption of 5.5 percent. The growth assumption was clearly far too optimistic at the time it was adopted."*

'Best Practice' Budget Process			Current Practice in Croatia	
Type of Analysis	Description	Responsible Organization	Responsible Organization	Analysis Performed
	CCG and LGUs spending. Having clearly defined roles between national and subnational governments is key.			
Organiza-tional	Given the sectoral policies, this analysis focuses on how best to distribute funds within sectors and functions among the government institutions that execute programs and policies (e.g., M.of Health). Included in this analysis is an examination of organizational issues (e.g., health programs or spending that occurs through different Ministries, or health policy objectives carried out across organizational boundaries). Organizational and programmatic performance measures should be included. Issues of effectiveness and efficiency are factored into this analysis. Also, factor into decisions any results from internal, external, or management audits, program evaluations, academic research, etc.	MoF or Economy. Implicitly also done by each organization, though each organization usually does not focus on allocations between ministries, but on a bottom-up total for each ministry's own programs. May also be done by professional staff of legislature, or by staff of BCs.	Implicitly in each spending ministry.	No systematic analysis performed at MoF. No ministry-wide analysis.
Budget Examina-tion	Traditional 'green-eye-shade' budget reviews. Scrutiny of detailed office and program requests from subordinate organizations, including reconciliation of requests with ceilings. Can also focus on the programs and activities methods (the means used to attain a given objective, such as regulation, direct service provision, grants, etc.). Emphasis on effectiveness and efficiency. Also examines organizational issues (number of staff, budget for salaries, average pay rates, equipment purchases). Includes project reviews, capital and non-capital spending.	Budget office (usually within MoF or MoE), and each ministry. May also be performed to some extent by committees or legislative organizat.; can be organizational or issue-oriented (e.g., travel expenses, administrative expenses)	None.	No. Spending ministries do some input analysis, though primarily by using the level of inputs from the prior year as the basis for budget requests. Budget document sent to Parliament is organized by broad organizational units rather than programs, so it is not readily amenable to program analysis.

Source: Staff.

Recommendations

- Collect economic forecasts from several leading private and public sector agencies to provide a better basis for judging government forecasts;

- Amend Budget Law to require this type of transparency on the economic estimates underlying the budget.

More explicit analytical materials should be prepared regarding the sectoral and functional allocation of public resources. This should include assessments of the relative returns to additional sectoral investments (e.g., additional economic benefits from additional spending in education or infrastructure), whether the nation is attaining desired objectives in each function or sector, and whether such results are being attained as efficiently as possible (e.g., does Croatia spend more per capita on education and achieve the same results as neighboring countries). For initially improving resource allocation decisions, it is easiest to start with the sectoral/functional analysis, and perhaps broad organizational analysis.

Recommendations

- Improve sectoral analysis underlying the budget;

- In the short-run, use international technical assistance to fill analytical gaps.

Budget examination, also frequently referred to as budget and program analysis, should make use of all available data in financial documents and databases, information from internal and external audits, performance information, and relevant academic or policy research, to assess and recommend funding levels for programs and activities (Box 3.4 for some of the assessments that should be considered when determining new budget levels for programs). In Croatia, no organization is responsible nor performs budget and program analysis. Currently, budget analysis focuses on incremental spending differences relative to the previous year and the annual budget ceiling. More comprehensive financial assessments should be made and factored into funding recommendations.

Recommendations

- Develop the analytical capacity of the budget office staff (training).

- Reorganize the budget office to assign specific Ministries or sectors to budget office staff so that they develop program and policy expertise in these areas and expand the staff with analytical skills.

- Use analytical materials and options, including written policy papers, as part of the budget development process.

- Establish the budget office in the Budget Law, and designate its responsibilities, in order to highlight the importance of analysis and the work of the budget office.

The provision of information to decision-makers and the public most commonly occurs through the budget document, which is itself based on the *chart of accounts.* The nature and type of information included has an impact on transparency and the ability of information users to make rational decisions. The current budget is based primarily upon the current chart of accounts, with very little detail on programs or activities within Ministries. Decision-makers outside each ministry have little idea what the money is being used for, and what is being purchased.

For example, in the Ministry of Health, the total budget allocation is divided between two "programs", the Ministerial Office and the Red Cross. In the Year 2000 Budget, 99.8 percent of total Ministry of Health spending was in one 'program' (Ministerial Office). Within the Minister of Health Ministerial Office position:

- 66.3 percent of the year 2000 budget is identified as 'transfers to the health fund.' Under this heading, there is specification of what the transfers support.

- A further 27.8 percent goes for the acquisition, construction, and maintenance of capital assets. Here, there is no detail as to whether they are hospitals, laboratories, clinics, or why they are needed.

Box 3.3: Information to Factor into Budget Decisions

Prior Year Spending:
Did the Agency stay within its budget, and why not?
Did the agency spend all of its funds, and why not?
Was there one-time funding included in last years budget that should not be included again this year?
Current Year Spending:
Is the agency staying within its allotments, and why not?
Is the agency spending at a rate which will lead to over-spending, and what measures must be taken now to correct?
Policy Performance
Did the agency fulfill the policy directives for the prior year? Are they doing so for the current year?
Audit Results
Were there internal or external audits of the agency or its programs and activities last year or this year? What are the implications for funding? Did the agency make any corrections recommended in the audits?
Program Evaluations
Were there any program evaluations of the agency or Ministry completed since the last budget cycle? What were the results, and what are the implications for funding?
Other studies
Was there any academic or private researcher papers or studies published that have implications for funding, program structure, etc.?
Performance Assessment
Did productivity increase or decrease from the last budget cycle?
Did the activity or program attain planned outputs for the prior year? Why or why not?
Did average costs per output increase or decrease, and why?
What did the agency accomplish over the past year? Is it achieving its objectives or fulfilling its mission? What is the outcome of the activity?

Recommendation

- Divide the budget for each ministry into major agencies (organizations within the ministry), and subdivide each agency budget into major programs and activities (ideally, in alignment with ministry core activities).

The Croatian budget and budget process also do not make use of output data to begin linking inputs and outputs, which improves the ability to assess the results of public expenditures. The annual budget does not identify specific quantities of output or services provided at any level of detail. To begin to move away from input-based budgeting towards output-based budgeting, the budget request for each program should include some administrative, process, and output measures. Identification of what each years' budget 'buys' under each program helps policy officials assess what level of funding is necessary. It also allows useful indicators to be developed, such as average cost per unit of output (efficiency), or average cost per beneficiary. The objective of a performance management system is to allow evaluation of whether a public investment is achieving its intended results, and whether it is doing so efficiently.

Performance measurement is an important tool to manage an increasingly complex administrative apparatus, and to hold career bureaucrats and organizations accountable. While output information is only the first step towards performance measurement, it is an important step.

Recommendation

- Incorporate basic output measures into the annual budgets, aiding transparency and accountability, and beginning to link resources with results.

The MoF does not consider whether programs are *mandatory* or *discretionary* in nature when making final allocations, and neither do line Ministries when allocating funds within their budget ceiling. Thus, there is an inadequate interface between budget allocation and execution. For example, both the MoF and Ministry of Labor allocate less than estimated costs to social service organizations that deliver social assistance programs. Social service organizations are third-party program administrators, implementing current law and funded by the line ministry. These agencies do not have the authority to deny unilaterally benefits based on budget levels. If a client is eligible for unemployment or other assistance, the agency provides the benefit, irrespective of the budgeted funding level.

For such mandatory programs, there is a clear tension between program operation (and attendant spending) and budget levels. In the case of mandatory programs, the MoF and line ministry must either:

- Budget actual costs to prevent arrears from being incurred;

- Draft legislation modifying benefit levels or other program variables (means testing based on income) to assure the program spends to budget, and submit the legislation with the budget;

- Empower the responsible line ministry to undertake demand management measures to stay within budget, or

- Empower the responsible line ministry to change benefit levels and eligibility criteria by decree to match program expenditures to available budget resources in any given year.

Absent some differentiation between mandatory programs and discretionary activities in budget treatment, program arrears are all but guaranteed.

Recommendation

- Prohibit budgeting less than full cost for mandatory programs unless specific legislation that will alter the program to meet available resources is drafted and transmitted with the annual budget.

A multi-year framework can improve decision-making by explicitly considering the multi-year implications of current and proposed spending, and identify issues today that must be addressed to maintain the multi-year public resource policies of the Government. A multi-year budget framework entails:

- Multi-year economic estimates;

- Multi-year budget revenue and expenditure estimates;

- Multi-year sectoral resource envelopes setting over-all policy for sectoral spending;

- Evaluation of current and proposed new spending in light of sectoral and public sector resource objectives.

Croatia has many of the basic components for implementing a multi-year framework, including multi-year economic and public sector estimates. Sectoral resource envelopes are prepared only a very aggregate level without any assessments of the relative returns to additional sectoral investments, or sector analysis done. And, while some new spending is evaluated in light of its impact on overall government resource limits, it is not clear this is undertaken systematically or for all spending. Another problem is the non-obligatory aspect of the multi-year framework. In the 2000 budget process, Parliament for the first time received a multi-year fiscal forecast with the budget document, though the discussion of the novel approach was limited. The document was considered to be only an academic attempt to frame the discussion of future budgets, without any binding or bounding decision-choices of the Government or for the Parliament. With the recent Wage Policy proposal for the period 2001-2003, Government itself has already proven the weakness of multi-year planning. The multi-year framework assumed a nominal public sector wage bill freeze, and the new wage policy exceeds that nominal freeze, with no offsetting savings.

Recommendation

- Develop an explicit multi-year framework to improve financial decision-making.

BUDGET EXECUTION, INTERNAL CONTROL AND AUDITING

Expenditure Control

One of the most important issues that should be addressed under budget execution, and to a lesser extent, budget formulation, is the level of detail to which funds are controlled. Currently, the Parliament passes budgets to the "third level" of the chart of accounts:

- Level 1 (skupina): #100 Current Expenditures;

- Level 2 (podskup): #100-10 Personal Emoluments;

- Level 3 (odjeljak): #100-10-010 Gross Salaries and Wages.

Each itemization of expenditure at Level 3 is a budget 'position,' with its own identification number. Spending is controlled against these positions. A typical 'agency' or office within a ministry will have four positions for personnel expenses: gross wages and salaries; allowances; employer's contributions (for benefits); and, other employee allowances (e.g., commuting allowance, retirement severance payment). Similarly, for material costs (supplies, etc.), an office will have eight or more positions: energy, public utilities, and other services; office supplies; other small inventory; communications expenses; information media expenses (e.g., printing); travel expenses; insurance expenses; staff education expenses; and, rental expenses. The current chart of accounts also allows up to 9 'third-level' categories for maintenance expenses, two categories for production-related expenses, and so on.

This level of detailed control is unnecessary, and more important, is inefficient. It is counterproductive for *controlling* expenditures for a number of reasons:[78]

- This level of control inhibits Ministries and agencies from managing their resources to accomplish their mission. Each ministry must have some managerial flexibility to choose the means through which they will accomplish their mission and the current detailed level of control essentially freezes in place the current method of operations;

- No agency can know in advance exactly how much it will spend on utilities, rent, office supplies, travel, etc. These are *estimates*. Agencies need some flexibility as actual workload changes;

- Spending control should be designed so that agencies can stay within their budgets, while accomplishing their mission. The system should allow agencies to spend

---

[78] Even if this level of detail (or greater detail) is desired for *reporting* expenses, it is counterproductive as a *control* approach.

more on office supplies, and less on other small inventory, if they choose to do so as long as their total spending remains within the budget limit;

- The budget law allows Ministries to transfer up to 5 percent of a position to other positions within the ministry (with Minister of Finance approval). However, this generates enormous paperwork and information processing burdens for each agency and ministry, as well as for the MoF. Enormous human resources are consumed in this process, for no apparent benefit;

- For transfers greater than 5 percent, a ministry sends a request to the Government. If approved, it is sent to the Parliament for approval. This, in turn, also ties up Parliament to effect a transfer from utilities to office supplies within a particular ministry.

Recommendation

- Negotiate with Parliament a new system of expenditure control that focuses on larger aggregations of funds, perhaps Level 2 (include the new level of control in a new budget law). More detailed reports could still be provided to Parliament for informational but not for control purposes.

Budget Execution

Under the current cash-based budget structure of Croatia, the functions of budget execution and cash management are merged. Budget execution is the implementation of the budget as passed by Parliament, and involves:

- A policy oversight component to assure Government and Parliamentary policy as contained in the budget are honored;

- Control over the rate of spending (allotments) to assure budget totals are honored;

- Managing cash balances so that government financial obligations are paid in a timely manner; and,

- Accurate and timely recording of expenditures in the accounting system.

The current budget execution function is divided among several offices, with no office assigned the lead for coordinating the entire process:

- The Budget Consolidation Office develops allotments (prepared by the Ministries), and processes transfers between budget positions;

- The Budget Execution Department processes payment orders from the Ministries;

- The Institute for Payments (ZAP) actually makes the payments, and records General Ledger entries;

- The MoF Accounting Department receives ZAP reports, and maintains a General Ledger.

Under the current system, each ministry submits its financial plans for the year, which is based on the "agreement" reached in budget preparation. These financial plans are modified to reflect the cash position of the Government, and become the basis for budget execution (payments order processing) by the Budget Execution Department (BED). Then, the BED practices cash rationing—limiting the payments to available cash balances. There is no monitoring or control of commitments, which all but guarantees the build-up of arrears. Adopting modified accrual budgeting and accounting, and commitment controls, as recommended earlier in this paper, is strongly recommended.

Introducing commitment budgeting allows the separation of cash management from spending control, and can allow the Government to develop contracting and procurement policies that improve the efficient use of public funds. The current emphasis on cash rationing appears to hinder some longer-term contracts that, if negotiated properly, could result in savings.

There is also a need for a Treasury Office. Currently, the MoF is taking steps to implement the Office. Adopting a Treasury Consolidated Fund (frequently referred to as a treasury single account) is also strongly recommended. The MoF is also taking steps in this regard, and completion of this project at the earliest possible time is encouraged. It is important to note that while a single treasury account is very important, and will improve cash management; it is not likely to solve the current arrears problem. Most of the current arrears stem from over-commitment of funds, not poor cash management.

Internal Control and Auditing: Overview

As noted earlier, Croatia's internal control and auditing functions are assigned to the line ministries.[79] The MoF has established detailed requirements for internal control and auditing, and the MoF's responsibility for budget supervision (internal auditing) is assigned to the BED.[80] The Budget Supervision Office (BSO) currently does not assess the adequacy of internal controls at the other ministries. Each Minister is responsible for internal control within his or her ministry and for internal control and auditing of all spending agencies within the competence of his or her Ministry.

The Ministry of Finance's Budget Supervision Office acts as the government-wide internal auditor. The Office was founded in 1996 and is currently organized under the Assistant Minister for Budget Execution in the MoF. The BSO prepares an annual audit work plan. The BSO employs four auditors (including the head of the office). The BSO is in charge of monitoring legal usage of budget revenues and expenditures, and advising on regulations affecting state expenditure. The Office inspects accounting and financial documents. Coverage of audits include all revenues, including ministry own revenues, transfers, budget funds, fees, etc. The responsibility of the budget inspector's office encompasses LGs, EBFs, and public

---

[79] Article 38 of the Budget Law of 1994 (Official Gazette Number 92/94) establishes this decentralized structure.
[80] See, the Regulations on Budget Supervision and Internal Control issued in October 1996 by the MoF.

enterprises; however, staff shortage induced the BSO to prioritize EBFs and to leave LGs and public enterprises unattended.

The BSO prepares reports for the MoF on its audit activities. Every six months, it prepares a work summary report. These reports include recommendations on improvements to the BSO and internal audit function. Also, after every inspection, the budget supervisors produce a report of findings and recommendations. The report is first given to the supervised Ministry, which can object, comment or correct the report. The BSO evaluates the Ministry input and can amend, as necessary, the report. The supervised Ministry must sign the report to acknowledge they have received and read it. The signed report then goes to the MoF, with a copy voluntarily sent to the State Audit Office (SAO).[81] If irregularities are found, the final report goes to the inspected Ministry, the Deputy Minister of Finance, the Assistant Minister for Budget Execution, the Assistant Minister for Budget Formulation, the SAO, as well as the appropriate enforcement authority (tax administration, finance police, state prosecutor).

The BSO has performed follow-up audits to assess whether irregularities identified in previous audits have been corrected. However, limited staff minimize the Offices ability to perform follow-up work. The Office is also unable to follow-up with enforcement agencies to determine whether penalties have in fact been assessed when recommended. Finally, the BED and Budget Consolidation Department do not use their influence to enforce BSO findings or push for corrections of irregularities.

The BSO does cooperate with the SAO, and frequently consults with them. Whereas the SAO looks only at over-all operations or spending for the past year, the BSO looks at current spending, usually one line item at a time, and goes very deep.

None of the sampled Ministries and EBFs had a working internal audit office. Internal audit offices had been formally established, but are yet to be staffed. Ministries reported they had initiated some internal control mechanisms, such as separation of duties in issuing payment orders, but lacked any guidance as to what steps to take in this regard.

Recommendations

- Amend the Budget Law to formally establish the BSO within the MoF. The BSO should be somewhat independent to pursue its mission, and report to the Minister or Deputy Minister of Finance. It should also be strengthened with additional staff and resources to properly carryout its duties.

- Conduct budget supervision audits through to the end user or recipient of funds, until internal auditing and control are institutionalized in government.

- Focus the BSO's activities on ex-post audits, with particular attention to evaluating the internal control and audit functions within each Ministry until such time as these functions are well established and operating effectively.

---

[81] The BSO is required to send the SAO only reports with findings of major irregularities.

- Develop and issue guidance and standards for Ministry internal control and audit functions to assure quality and consistency, including developing professional standards of training for Ministry auditors.

- Amend the budget law to strengthen the penalties for over-spending budgeted resources and violating the budget law, and clearly assign to the BSO the responsible for monitoring compliance with the law and assigning penalties.

- Transfer staff and resources from other ministry activities to establish functioning internal control structures in each ministry.

Program evaluation is a deeper examination of specific programs to assess their effectiveness in achieving objectives and outcomes. Croatia does not have a mechanism for conducting deeper program evaluations. Program evaluations usually occur outside the normal budget cycle, but they are integrally linked to the budgets. The selection of which programs to perform deeper evaluations of usually arises in the context of budget preparation and enactment. If questions are raised about program accomplishments and effectiveness that cannot be answered quickly during budget debates, these programs should be selected for deeper analysis. Deeper evaluations identify programmatic weaknesses, suggest improvements and enhancements, and are an important tool for program management and budget allocation. The results of program evaluations are incorporated into future year's budget decisions.

Recommendation

- Create, as a medium term objective, a capacity for undertaking deeper program evaluations. This need not require the establishment of a new organization, but a pool of budgetary resources for use in commissioning evaluations by academic or private sector researchers would fill this need. To protect the independence of the evaluations, the MoF should commission the studies, and competitively bid the work. These external audits should be extended to include management and performance assessments.

EXTERNAL REVIEW: THE ROLE OF PARLIAMENT AND THE SUPREME AUDIT INSTITUTION

The Role of Parliament: Budget Passage

The Constitution gives the Croatian Parliament (Sabor) authority to adopt the budget, as well as the primary responsibility for adopting legislation.[82] Since the recent constitutional amendment (2001) the Sabor became a unicameral assembly formed by the Chamber of Deputies (Zastupnicki dom).[83] Under its own internal rules, the Sabor organizes into committees of

---

[82] See, Constitution of the Republic of Croatia (1990), Articles 80, 81, and 91; and amendment to the Constitution (2001) articles 80/90.

[83] The new configuration replaces the previous bi-cameral structure; also formed by the Chamber of Counties (Zupanijski dom).

jurisdiction to address functional or sectoral issues; one of which is the Committee on Budget and Finance, or simply, the Budget Committee (BC).

The Budget Committee (BC) has an important role in the budget process. Budget bills are referred to the BC.[84] Other relevant sectoral committees (e.g., health) have an informal role in the process receiving a copy of the proposed Budget for comment on their sections. The views of these other committees, however, are advisory and non-binding on the BC. The BC does not use the SAO during budget formulation.[85] Under current Sabor rules, the BC proposes a change to the Government, the Government accepts or rejects the proposal, and sends the budget back to the BC. The Sabor cannot consider the budget until the BC has rendered an opinion. If no opinion is rendered by the BC, the Sabor cannot vote on the budget. If the BC gives a negative opinion, the Sabor receives the budget and committee opinion, and decides whether to follow the Government or BC view.

The Sabor is not consulted by the Government or involved in budget formulation until the Budget is formally proposed by Government. Substantive Parliament-Government negotiations do not occur until the budget formally arrives from Government. The current budget submission from the Government only includes a broad policy statement and tables of numbers. There is no explanatory material on budget or policy changes, and therefore it is very difficult for the Sabor and BC to ascertain what is happening. The most detailed section of the current budget—lists of capital projects—reportedly receives the most attention from MP's during budget debates.

The Role of Parliament: Budget Execution

In Parliamentary systems, the legislature, and especially the Public Accounts Committee (budget), play an important role in financial accountability, monitoring budget execution. In Croatia, however, the Sabor's effectiveness in monitoring budget execution is limited due to: limited information made available to the Sabor; limited capacity to utilize information; and deferring to the executive in financial matters. The Sabor receives two reports on execution each year, one mid-year and one year-end. If the budget is out of balance during the year, theoretically the Sabor could take direct action. In practice, however, the Sabor follows the Government's lead and consequently is not in a position to serve as an instrument of accountability. Ex-post, the Sabor receives the closing accounts bill, submitted after the end of the fiscal year, and the report of the SAO. But with limited analytical capacity of its own, there is little the Sabor can do except approve the closing accounts bill.

Overall, the Sabor needs to develop capacity to participate more actively and become an instrument for accountability. Currently, the low level of committee staffing means that the Parliament has effectively no independent expert advice supporting its involvement in the budget process. Neither the BC nor the Parliament has sufficient staff support to seriously analyze or engage the Government on substantive policy issues in the budget process. The only interaction

---

[84] The current BC consists of nine members: the chair, and eight other MP's. Committee staff consists of four members: one secretary, one budget expert, and two other staff.

[85] In Hungary, the Parliament asks the SAO for an opinion on the economic and technical assumptions underlying the proposed budget, but does not ask for policy advice. Even this technical support does not sit well with Hungarian SAO staff.

between the committee and SAO is the annual audit of the prior year submitted to the Parliament. The BC provides comments on the audit before it goes to Parliament; but it cannot request special audits by the SAO or special studies. The Sabor needs better budget data and more detailed commentary to understand what is happening in each Ministry, where changes are being proposed and why.

Recommendations

- Strengthen the staff of the BC with several professionals dedicated to public expenditure analysis;

- Improve the quality and content of the annual budget submission to the Sabor to enable a fuller debate on the budget (more user friendly).

- Take steps to enhance Sabor's knowledge and background on budget, through, inter-alia, brief (1-2 day) training for MP's on the budget, budget process, basic statutes, etc.

External Audit and Evaluation: The Role of the State Audit Office

The SAO is the Supreme Audit Institution of the Republic of Croatia, and reports to the Chamber of Deputies (Zastupnicki dom). The SAO follows the audit office model of supreme audit institutions, and was established by the SAO Act of 1993. The Office itself was established in 1994, and this is its 6th year of operation. The SAO adopted the auditing standards of the International Organization of Supreme Audit Institutions (INTOSAI) as their standards, as well as the principles of the 1977 Lima Declaration.

The SAO produces an annual audit plan that is submitted to Parliament for approval and has the authority to audit all entities receiving public funds. This includes Ministries and agencies, local governments (county and municipal), EBFs, central bank expenditures (not open market operations), public enterprises, and the privatization office's expenditures (not the privatization process or outcomes). Parliament has the authority to change the plan or to direct the focal points of audits, but to date has not exercised this authority.

The SAO is authorized to have 291 staff. Seventy three are in the Zagreb office, which is the headquarters of the SAO, and 218 staff are in the 20 county SAO offices. There are currently 45 vacancies in the SAO. The Zagreb office focuses its direct audit work on the CG. County SAO offices focus mainly on local government audits, thought they may review regional activities of central government Ministries. SAO employees must have an advanced degree in economics or law, pass the civil service exam, and also pass a licensing exam for state auditors. The SAO also has the authority to hire other specialists with advanced degrees (e.g., engineers or physicians), but has not done so to date. At present, roughly 90 percent of SAO employees are economists and 10 percent lawyers.

The SAO produces one consolidated annual report to Parliament of audit findings, including findings from local government audits. The county and municipal governments also receive an annual audit report, but only those audits dealing with their governments programs and expenditures. The SAO has no prosecutorial authority. If the SAO finds wrong-doing, they can only report it to the Parliament and Government. The MoF Financial Police and State Prosecutor's Office are responsible for investigation and prosecution. The Sabor can also hold hearings on findings.

The SAO has broad authority to conduct financial and performance audits of Government. SAO staff view their core function as expenditure audits and therefore, they focus the audits mainly on financial and compliance issues, looking at the accuracy of financial records. The SAO audit programs have focused on adherence to current law and on the larger expenditures. SAO staff do report some problems with adherence to current budget and financial laws. SAO staff report that they generally report instances of non-compliance in audit reports. However, in recent years, given the fiscal problems of the Government, the SAO staff have been 'understanding' and not cited failures to comply with current law regarding arrears, over-spending, unplanned expenditures, limits on re-allocation between line items, and other issues.

According to SAO staff, roughly 75 percent of SAO findings are corrected by the Government within one year. The SAO does include an assessment of Government's response to prior year audit findings in their annual reports.

Recommendations

- Focus on compliance and financial audits in the short term. Management and performance audits should be a longer-term goal of the SAO, after the current Croatian public expenditure system has further developed and stabilized.

- Cite deviations from the current law and discontinue practice of 'understanding' non-compliance with current law. This is essential to maintain the SAO's own credibility and also maintain the integrity of the financial management system.

CURRENT BUDGET LAW ASSESSMENT

The current Croatian Budget Act, enacted in 1994, provides a sound basis upon which to build. It includes a general calendar for the budget process, some definition of roles and responsibilities of key actors in the process, and some technical definitions of relevant terms. It also covers many of the issues that should be covered in a budget law, such as how unliquidated obligations should be handled in subsequent years.

This Report has identified a number of areas where amendments changes to the Budget Law may be desirable. The degree of detail or breadth of provisions to include in a law versus subsidiary legal instruments (e.g., decrees) depends heavily on the legal system of each country, as well as its socio-legal tradition. Croatia has a civil law tradition, where it is not unusual for laws to contain implementing details. The law also seems to have an important signaling component in Croatia. For example, in implementing a Single Treasury Account, the MoF decree is not taken as seriously as a law would be. It appears that whether the weight of the entire Government is behind a policy (law) versus the weight of one Ministry (decree) bears some relation to the success of implementation. Therefore, this final section discusses general categories of difficulties that arise under the current law are:

- Provisions of the current law that are not implemented.

- Key recommended changes to the current Budget Law.

Some specific issues regarding provisions in the current Budget law that are not being adequately implemented are:

- Article 5 (3) states that *"In the event that during the fiscal year a regulation is adopted having the effect of decreasing the planned revenues and receipts or increasing the planned expenditure, a decision shall be passed at the same time determining additional revenues needed to balance the budget."* This is an excellent provisions which requires actions taken during the year, but has not been implemented;

- Article 13 (2.2) requires spending agencies to provide three-year (multi-year) budget estimates to the Minster of Finance. Article 18 (2) requires multi-year estimates be provided to the Sabor. Multi-year approaches allow improved planning and financial stability. However, this has not been implemented in practice.

- Article 29 (2) states that *"Any financial obligation not settled by December 31 of the current year shall be settled from the earmarked funds approved in the budget of the following fiscal year."* Explicitly addressing how arrears or unliquidated obligations will be addressed is a sound element of a budget law. However, in practice, this has resulted in the central budget being responsible for handling arrears, and not the agency responsible for incurring them.

- Article 2 (r) defines the Treasury as including budget planning. It is unusual for the Treasury function to include budget formulation (planning), and would also detract from the primary focus on cash and debt management that is the core function of a Treasury office.

There are several areas where amendments to the Budget Law could be used to clarify roles and responsibilities, clarify terms and processes, and generally strengthen the public finance system. The key principles underlying these proposed revisions are:

- Bringing all sources and uses of funds in the budget;

- Including all CG entities, and only CG entities;

- Adopting modified accrual accounting; and,

- Improving the transparency of budget decisions and implementation.

Include all sources and uses of funds in the budget. Government officials, Members of Parliament, and Citizens cannot make informed decisions on government spending unless they have a complete picture of the total resources available to the Government and to individual

Ministries and programs. Excluding some categories of revenue or expenditure from the budget gives decision-makers a false impression of resources, and opens opportunities for misuse of funds.

All funds should be subject to the same regulations, controls, and standards of accountability. This includes grants (all sources), own revenues, transfers between Ministries, carry-over of funds from prior years, etc. Ministries can still be allowed to keep 100 percent of own revenues, but these must now be declared in the budget, and some sources appropriated by the Parliament to be spent.[86]

Include all CG entities, and only CG entities. This means including all organizations that are established as agents of the CG, and subject to government control and oversight. As defined in the current budget law, budget beneficiaries include ministries and other bodies of national administration and other organizations funded from the budget. Technically, this could include a non-governmental research organization that receives 1 HRK from the budget. Such organizations do not belong on the government accounts. The Government should be able to audit the funds received from the national budget for appropriate use, but otherwise does not want this organization and its employees showing-up as government entities.

Under this principle, include EBFs/organizations (even if allowed to govern their own affairs through a board), but exclude LGs and non-governmental grantees (the latter can still be subject to audit requirements and requirements that they use funds for the appropriated purpose). This means changing the definition of 'budget beneficiary' as contained in the current budget law.

Some possible tests for determining whether an organization belongs in the government budget or government sector are:

- The organization was created by a formal Government act (law, decree, regulation, etc.);

- The specific mission, purpose or objectives of the organization are established in law or decree, and the organization carries out its duties with the authority of the Government;

- The employees of the organization are government (civil service) employees, or the organization was granted its own personnel system (pay rates, job classifications, benefits, etc.);

- The chief executive and/or board of directors of the organization are appointed by the Government.

---

[86] A provision should be added allowing the Minister of Finance to authorize commitments against own revenues above budget estimates when revenues exceed those estimated in the budget. This covers cases where a grant or loan may be received after the budget has been approved.

Adopt Modified Accrual Accounting

Revenues should be recorded when measurable and available, while expenditures are recognized when incurred (regardless of whether actually paid). For example, 'expenditures' would definitely be recognized for goods or services received though no invoice was received or cash paid. They might also be recorded when a contract is signed, though no actual goods or services have been received (U.S. Federal Government). It depends on how conservative the Government wants to be in controlling spending. Modified accrual captures commitments to receive goods and services, and will help control the arrears problem in most agencies. However, modified accrual *per-se* is not likely to have much effect on Health Insurance or Pension Fund arrears. The structural imbalance between revenues and expenses, and inability of these EBFs to control expenditures, assures continued arrears in those areas.

This shift to modified accrual accounting is likely to have a significant effect on capital spending. The cost of construction should be fully accounted for in the year in which budgeted, instead of partial funding of many new projects. This assures funding to approved projects, allows contracting for the entire project (with potential cost savings), and helps assure those projects undertaken are completed and can add to national welfare. This will help alleviate concerns expressed by the staff of the MoF regarding capital project completion. New projects are initiated, with insufficient attention to completion of current projects. Data available in the MoF should allow more careful review of recent spending patterns by project, as well as estimation of the impact of modified accrual on the pattern of capital spending.

Adopt Sound Financial Practices

This involves implementation more than the law, per se. Generally, it means operating national finances consistent with common or preferred international practice. For example, commitments and debt of the Government are only settled in cash, not in barter, shares of companies, etc. If the Government requires cash, the Treasury issues formal debt, or perhaps assets or government shares in private corporations are sold on the market. Cash thus raised is used to liquidate obligations. Where these practices are not in fact followed, it is advisable to incorporate them into the budget law.

Transparency

While some of the foregoing principles relate to transparency, there is also a need to focus directly on transparency in drafting the budget to assure budget processes are clear, responsibility and accountability clearly assigned, and information provided meets the needs of budget users and decision-makers (including Citizen's).

LATEST DEVELOPMENTS

Since the presentation of this Report to the Croatian authorities, the Government of Croatia has started implementing several of the recommendations embedded in this Chapter. In this regard, an important first step was taken this year, with the inclusion of the Pension Fund within the budget, starting from July 1st; this has contributed to greatly enhance the comprehensiveness of the budget. In addition, in line with the Report's recommendations, the

Budget Internal Control Department has been established, and the Parliamentary Committee for Budget and Finance has been strengthened with the addition of six qualified professionals from a pool of groups consisting of labor unions, the employers' association and the chamber of commerce, academicians and private auditors' representatives. Furthermore, to improve parliamentarian involvement in the budget process, a Citizen's Guide to the Budget was prepared in late 2000. Additional measures to strengthen the budget process, which are expected to be adopted are: the inclusion of the Health Fund within the budget from January 2002; and the introduction of modified accrual budgeting and the inclusion of own revenues –previously excluded- for all budget users, starting with the next budget process. Finally, new charts of accounts are being prepared to allow the introduction of both accrual budgeting and the inclusion of previously un-captured own revenues.

ANNEX A: FISCAL SUSTAINABILITY

This section discusses the sustainability of fiscal policy in Croatia. As a lead-in to the discussion, the first subsection overviews some issues regarding fiscal sustainability that pertain specifically to Croatia. The second subsection provides a review of the concept of fiscal sustainability and how it relates to the task of projecting an economy's future inflation path. It is followed by an analysis of the situation in Croatia, which concludes that the current fiscal situation is far from what is sustainable in the long run. Given this conclusion, the obvious question is "How can Croatia restore itself to a situation with sound finances and better prospects for economic performance in the future?" The answer to this question lies in a well-designed fiscal reform that would permit better-coordinated fiscal and monetary policy. Such a reform would improve Croatia's prospects for sustained growth with low inflation.

ISSUES OF SPECIFIC RELEVANCE TO CROATIA

Usually discussions of fiscal sustainability center around the (i) how to measure the Government's deficit, (ii) the size of the Government's debt, (iii) the ability of the Government to raise seignorage revenue, and (iv) the likely path of future economic growth. A number of important issues of very specific relevance to Croatia need to be discussed.

Measuring the Deficit

In Croatia, most published statistics relating to the deficit refer to the cash deficit of the CG and the CCG. The use of cash deficits in assessing sustainability is not a major problem unless the cash deficit deviates substantially from the deficit on an accrual basis.[87] Unfortunately, in the Croatian case, there are substantial differences between these two deficit concepts due to arrears on government payment obligations. Estimates for 1998 and 1999 suggest that the accrual-basis budget of the CG differed from the cash-basis budget, in both years, by about 1.9 percent of GDP.

In Croatia, privatization is an important source of government finance. Thus, a second important issue in deficit measurement is whether to include privatization receipts as part of government revenue. From an *economic* standpoint, there is no compelling reason to think of privatization receipts as income. To see this, note that the Government's deficit, measured in real terms, should correspond to the change in the Government's real net worth. Suppose the Government's real deficit, excluding privatization receipts is zero. If the Government sells an asset, in exchange for cash, this cash can be used to retire some debt (since there is a zero deficit). In this example, there is no change in the Government's net worth because government assets and liabilities have decreased by the same amount. In a situation where the Government does have a deficit, the sale of an asset represents a source of finance (not revenue), as does the acquisition of a debt obligation.

---

[87] Normally the two would differ by the change in the Government's float in its account at the central bank, and this would typically average to zero over time.

This analysis is very significant for Croatia because once privatization revenues are excluded this substantially changes one's view of the overall fiscal picture in recent years. In 1997, 1998 and 1999, the Government obtained privatization revenues of about 0.6, 1.6 and 4.4 percent of GDP respectively. The net effect is that rather than having an average accrual-basis deficit of about 2.2 percent of GDP across these years, the government actually ran an accrual-basis deficit of 4.4 percent of GDP, on average.

Despite the fact that privatization receipts should be excluded from the calculation of the government's deficit, they may be nonetheless crucial to the budgetary process. Consider a situation where the government needs to finance a deficit of a given size. As demonstrated above, this deficit could be financed by the acquisition of debt, or by the sale of an asset. If the Government had a large gross debt position, it might run into a short-run borrowing constraint whereby it could not take on any more debt. On the other hand, it could meet its financing needs through privatization. In this sense, privatization could be critical to the very short-run sustainability of the government's fiscal position. On the other hand, selling valuable assets during a period of crisis is hardly likely to yield the best price on those assets if the Government's bargaining position has any effect on the price.

The Stock of Government Debt

Fiscal sustainability calculations are forward looking. They ask a simple question: "Given the government's initial stock of debt, what primary surplus position would the government need to maintain to prevent its stock of debt from spiraling out of control?"[88] The projected primary surplus that emerges in the answer to this question depends on the estimate of initial debt.

What should be included in an economically meaningful measure of the initial stock of net debt? Gross debt should include all government obligations. Gross assets should include all *conceivably liquid* government assets. Why the caveat of *conceivably liquid*? The measure of assets should include those assets that could be used as a source of financing. On the other hand, it should exclude those assets the government would need in order to generate the projected fiscal surpluses. Some simple examples are equipment and buildings needed in order to house government offices. More subtly, one would have to exclude any public sector corporations the government intended to keep on its books indefinitely. Obviously, for a country like Croatia, with a very large public sector, this measurement issue could be very important. It will arise, again, below.

Another important issue in measuring Croatia's stock of debt is that because of arrears, conventional debt measures–which reflect the outstanding stock of formal government debt instruments (e.g., Treasury bills)–do not accurately reflect the government's debt position. Fortunately, estimates of the government's stock of outstanding arrears exist.

Finally, there is the difficult question of how to deal with contingent liabilities. These come in two forms: (i) liabilities that were contingent, have become actual liabilities, but have not been securitized or, in some cases, have not been formally recognized in the budget and (ii)

---

[88] A formal definition of what is meant by spiraling out of control is discussed below. Formally, debt is "spiraling out of control" when the Government's financial behavior is equivalent to a Ponzi scheme.

liabilities that are still contingent, such as government-guaranteed debt issued by the private sector.[89] Croatia has liabilities in both categories. For example, the banking crisis of 1998-99 led to government intervention in the financial sector. Governments acquire fiscal costs in such crises, either by paying out funds to bank creditors, or through the cost of bank recapitalization. Estimates of these fiscal costs should be included in the stock of government debt, yet producing such estimates is fraught with difficulty. They depend on assumptions about the government's willingness to fully bail out creditors and the extent to which the assets of failed banks can be recovered.

Seignorage Revenue

One source of government revenue is seignorage.[90] The more seignorage revenue a government can raise, the larger its primary deficit can be, for the same level of indebtedness. However, seignorage is raised through the expansion of the monetary base. Hence, the government's ability to raise seignorage is tempered by two facts. First, heavy reliance on seignorage is inflationary. Second, seignorage is limited by the private sector's demand for money, which is likely to be decreasing in the nominal interest rate. So, even if a government is willing to pay the price of high inflation, it may find that its ability to raise seignorage is limited, because as the inflation rate rises, the nominal interest rate will rise, and the public's willingness to hold money balances will decline.

Seignorage is further limited when currency substitution is widespread. When, as in Croatia, the public has access to foreign currency deposits, or has even limited access to foreign capital markets, the currency favored in transactions can easily switch from domestic to foreign currency. Other things equal, this suggests that in an economy like Croatia's, the public's demand for domestic currency may be sharply decreasing in the nominal interest rate especially if it reflects expected inflation. Thus, the Government's ability to raise seignorage may be very limited.

Economic Growth

An inherent problem with sustainability calculations is that they depend on assumptions about economic growth. Given that growth is very difficult to predict, this means that it is a major source of uncertainty in estimates of the sustainable primary surplus. Why is growth relevant? To see why, a simple example suffices. Imagine a country in which the operational deficit is zero.[91] This means that the country's real stock of debt is constant. However, if real GDP is rising, the country's stock of debt as a fraction of GDP will decline over time. From this example, it is clear that a country could have a rising real stock of debt, but it could be declining when expressed as a fraction of GDP. This would simply require that the real debt stock grew at a slower rate than the growth rate of real GDP. The faster the real growth rate, the higher the operational deficit that could be sustained.

---

[89] Presumably government-guaranteed debt issued by public sector entities would already be reflected in some measure of the public sector's stock of debt.

[90] Once the central bank is included in the definition of the public sector, seignorage revenue helps finance the budget even if the central bank does not directly supply seignorage proceeds to the Government.

[91] i.e., the primary deficit plus real interest payments equals zero.

The fact that growth is so important suggests that not all primary surpluses of the same magnitude will be created equal. For example, consider two economies with the same primary surplus of, say, 2 percent of GDP. In the first economy primary government spending equals 30 percent of GDP, and taxes equal 32 percent of GDP. In the second economy the surplus is achieved through primary government spending of 20 percent of GDP, and taxes equal to 22 percent of GDP. Since taxes are usually distorting, others things equal, one would expect the growth rate of the high spending-high tax economy to be lower.[92] Hence, its fiscal position would be less sustainable. Other things equal, Croatia fits into the high tax-high expenditure category. While it has plenty of potential for rapid growth, the substantial presence of the government in the economy works against this potential.

Concepts of Fiscal Sustainability

This section examines ways of phrasing the following question: "Are the government's fiscal and monetary policies sustainable?" It argues that this question should not be treated as equivalent to another: "Can the government finance itself?" The answer to this latter question is (almost) always "Yes," both in the short run and the long run. The distinction between the two questions lies in the fact that the first is more restrictive. For the government's policies to be sustainable they must not only be financed, they must be consistent with *desired* rates of growth and inflation.

Any government (consolidated with its central bank) is subject to an intertemporal budget constraint, or budget identity:

(1)   <u>nominal value of new debt = fiscal deficit – seignorage revenue</u>, where all variables are measured in local currency. Generally speaking, debt is not denominated in units of goods, rather, it is denominated in terms of units of domestic or foreign currency.[93] So the value of previously issued debt can change over time due to changes in the domestic price level and changes in the rate of exchange between domestic and foreign currency. As a result the change in the real value of government debt is determined according to

(2)   <u>increase in real debt = operational deficit – seignorage revenue</u>, where all variables are measured in units of goods. Correctly measured the operational deficit makes the following adjustments to the standard deficit: (i) it subtracts an inflation correction related to the fact that nominal interest payments on nonindexed domestic debt have an amortization component given by the inflation rate times the stock of such debt,[94] (ii) it subtracts a revaluation term that takes into account how changes in the exchange rate affect the value of outstanding foreign debt.[95]

---

[92] Unless, of course, the high tax country used less distorting methods of taxation and had a more growth- supportive spending program.
[93] The obvious exception is domestic debt indexed to the value of a commodity basket such as the consumer price index.
[94] Hence the inflation correction is given by $-\pi b$, where π is the inflation rate and b is the real stock of domestic nonindexed debt.
[95] The revaluation correction is $-(\pi-\delta)b^*$ where δ is the nominal rate of depreciation of the currency and b^* is the real stock of outstanding foreign debt. See the appendix for further details.

Definition 1: The Government's fiscal position is sustainable in the very short run if it is feasible for the government to finance its operational deficit; i.e., if it can raise sufficient seignorage revenue and debt finance to cover the deficit.

Over the longer run, such a definition of sustainability is clearly unsuitable because governments cannot run Ponzi schemes, at least not without compelling their citizens to hold government paper. This does not mean that governments have to pay off their debt (Buiter, 1989). Rather, it means that in the long run they must accumulate *real* debt at a rate lower than the real rate of interest—that is, they must amortize at least some small fraction of their debt.[96]

Effectively, the two adjustments made in moving to the operational deficit concept mean that the increase in real debt can be written as:

(3)   increase in real debt = primary deficit + real interest payments – seignorage

If one eliminates the possibility of a government-run Ponzi scheme, equation (3) leads to the present-value condition:

(4)   real value of government debt = present value of future $\begin{cases} \text{primary surpluses -} \\ \text{risk premiums +} \\ \text{seignorage revenues.} \end{cases}$

The "risk premiums" part of this equation simply reflects the fact that if the present value in equation (4) is computed using the world interest rate as the discount factor, this may not correspond to the effective real interest rate the Government pays on its debt. The Government may have to pay substantial risk premiums, on average, to borrow in the world capital market, and it may have to pay high real interest rates on its domestic debt.

Definition 2: The path of fiscal policy is sustainable in the long run if it is feasible for the government to raise enough seignorage revenue in the future to make (4) hold given (i) the current real value of government debt, (ii) the present value of future primary surpluses and (iii) the present value of the likely risk premiums it will have to pay on its debt.[97]

Of course, even this second definition of sustainability is less than fully suitable. After all, according to this definition, fiscal policy is described as sustainable even if the government uses large amounts of seignorage revenue to finance itself. In some countries the government may be able to raise substantial amounts of revenue through seignorage, but it will do this at the cost of high long-run inflation, with all of its negative consequences. This leads naturally to a third definition of sustainability:

---

[96] In a Ponzi scheme the Government would issue new debt to service the real interest bill on its existing debt and thus would accumulate debt at a rate equal to the real interest rate.

[97] A branch of the literature on fiscal and monetary policy (see, for example, Cochrane (2000), Sims (2000) or Woodford (2000)) argues that some version of (4) must always hold. In these *fiscal theories of the price level* the left-hand side of equation for is the ratio of the nominal value of government debt to the price level. The price level is treated as an endogenous variable that adjusts so that (4) holds exactly. Of course, this requires that the Government issues some nominal debt and that it does not use price fixing schemes such as a fixed exchange rate.

Definition 3: The path of fiscal policy satisfies a long-run sustainability condition if (4) is satisfied given (i) the current real value of government debt, (ii) the present value of future primary surpluses, (iii) zero risk premiums and (iv) fixed targets for long-run inflation and growth.

Below, this definition of fiscal sustainability is employed to analyze whether the fiscal situation in Croatia is sustainable. Before turning to this question, the next subsection relates the concept of fiscal sustainability to the determination of inflation.

INFLATION AND THE GOVERNMENT BUDGET CONSTRAINT

Why is inflation linked inextricably to the government's budget constraint? Suppose the government contemplates higher current or future spending or lower current or future taxes. Absent decreases in other forms of spending or increases in other forms of taxes, these changes in fiscal policy imply a decrease in the present value of future primary surpluses (one of the terms on the right hand side of equation [4]). Absent the ability to determine the risk premium on its own debt, the government must use some combination of (i) an immediate jump in the price level (discontinuous inflation) to devalue its nominal debt (this lowers the left-hand side of [4]) or (ii) future *increases* in the inflation rate to raise the value of its seignorage revenue (this raises the right-hand side of [4]).[98]

Equation (4) is also interesting in that it shows a certain irrelevance of the government's short-run decisions about how to finance its deficit. Borrowing rather than printing money does not change the amount of seignorage revenue the government will need in the long run, absent a fiscal reform. So while government decisions about when to borrow and when to print money will affect the path that inflation takes, they will not affect the total amount of seignorage that inflation must generate.[99]

It is this logic that led Sargent and Wallace (1980) to coin the phrase *unpleasant monetarist arithmetic*. Suppose that initially the government's fiscal and monetary policies are consistent with very low inflation. Then suppose that the government announces a new path for fiscal policy under which the primary surplus will be lower than under the previous policy regime. The government can keep inflation low in the short run, by borrowing, rather than printing money. However, the government cannot escape the logic of the lifetime budget constraint illustrated by equation (4). By maintaining low inflation in the short run the government simply raises the inflation rate that will be needed in the future to generate sufficient seignorage revenue to finance the change in fiscal policy. The argument is quite simple. By keeping initial inflation low, the bulk of the required seignorage revenue accrues in the more distant future. Hence it is discounted more when computing its present value. The longer raising

---

[98] Presumably the risk premium on government debt is determined by market forces, and is outside the Government's control. Also, if the Government has already exhausted all potential for increased seignorage revenue in the future, the only possible outcome is an immediate devaluation of its existing debt stock through a jump in the price level.

[99] This discussion is somewhat oversimplified since the pattern of government borrowing could affect the present value of the risk premium payments made by it.

seignorage is postponed, the more it will be discounted, and hence a greater flow of it will be required to balance the lifetime budget constraint.

The cost of a tight money policy in the short run is a loose money policy in the long run. There is only one policy consistent with persistently low inflation: if the government raises expenditure, it must raise the present value of future taxes; if it cuts taxes, it must cut the present value of future primary expenditure.

LONG RUN SUSTAINABILITY IN CROATIA

To estimate a sustainable *long run* path for fiscal policy in Croatia, consider the case where inflation is low and constant, at some rate π, output is growing along some steady state path at the rate, μ, and the government does not pay a risk premium over the world real interest rate, r. Assume, also, that in such a situation, there is a stable demand for base money given by:

(5) $m^d = (M^d/PY) = L(r+\pi)$

where M^d is the demand for nominal money balances, P is the price level, Y is the level of output, r is the real interest rate, π is the inflation rate, and $L(\cdot)$ is some decreasing function of the nominal interest rate $r+\pi$. In this case, the present value of seignorage revenue accruing to the government would be given by $(\pi+\mu)L(r+\pi)/(r-\mu)$, expressed as a fraction of GDP.

Suppose that in this long-run steady state the government also has constant levels of purchases and taxes net of transfers given by g and τ respectively, as a fraction of GDP. This implies that the present value of the Government's future primary surpluses is given by $(g-\tau)/(r-\mu)$. If the Government's initial debt is b_0, as a fraction of GDP, the sustainability condition implies that

(6) $g - \tau = (r-\mu)b_0 - (\pi+\mu)L(r+\pi)$.

What does this condition predict for Croatia? To make such a prediction some assumptions are required. The baseline assumptions made here are as follows:

1. Let b_0 be given by the 1999 level of public sector and public sector guaranteed debt, relative to GDP. I.e. let $b_0 = 0.545$.[100]

2. Let r be the sample average of the real interest rate in the period 1980–1999, as measured by the U.S. treasury bonds yield minus the rate of inflation of the U.S. GDP deflator.[101] That is, let $r = 0.055$.

---

[100] Notice that this baseline calculation leaves out (i) any marketable assets the Croatian Government might have, (ii) any assessment of contingent liabilities, (iii) non-government public sector debt, unless guaranteed by the Government and (iv) the reserves of the central bank (Hrk 23.1 billion at the end of 1999). Included in the debt figures are Hrk 8.6 billion (6 percent of GDP) in government arrears of the following forms: unpaid obligations of the Health Fund, promissory notes and floating debt.

[101] These are measured using the International Financial Statistics series 61. ZF–INTEREST:GOVT BOND YIELD (AVG YIELD TO MATURITY) and 99BIRZF–GDP DEFLATOR (1995=100)(const. national currency—seasonally adjusted by national compiler) for the United States.

3. Let the target long-run inflation and real growth rates correspond to the long-run values in the Government of Croatia's current 3-year planning documents. I.e., let $\pi = 0.035$ and let $\mu = 0.05$.

4. Let $L(r+\pi)$ be given by estimates of the long-run money demand function for Croatia, in the form of $L(r+\pi) = Ae^{-\eta(r+\pi)}$ with $A = 0.102$ and $\eta = 3.68$.

Given these assumptions, the estimated sustainable primary fiscal surplus is -0.3 percent of GDP. This comes from a combined estimated debt service cost of 0.3 percent of GDP, plus seignorage revenue of just 0.6 percent of GDP. In fact, money demand seems to be so elastic in Croatia that the *maximal* seignorage the government could raise is not much higher: seignorage is maximized, by a 22 percent inflation rate, at just 1 percent of GDP. This means that even in a high inflation environment the primary fiscal surplus could be no lower than -0.7 percent of GDP.

So far, this section's estimates of the sustainable fiscal surplus have corresponded to the case where inflation, real growth and the real interest rate are all constant. In this environment, if the Government holds the primary surplus fixed at the level indicated by equation (6), the real stock of debt will not only grow over time in a manner consistent with the no-Ponzi scheme condition. It will also grow at the rate of growth of GDP, so that the debt stock as a fraction of GDP will be constant.[102]

Of course, in the short-run, a government may face higher than long-run inflationary pressure, lower than long-run growth, and significantly higher than long-run real interest rates. Suppose a government facing these short-run difficulties chose to have a primary surplus given by (6). The inevitable consequence of this decision, according to equation (4), is that there would be higher inflation than the long-run target of 3.5 percent. This inflation could occur immediately, or in the future, but it would be unavoidable. In order to keep inflation under control, the government facing short-run difficulties would need to have higher primary surpluses than those that are sustainable in the long run. The next subsection turns to the issue of short run sustainability.

SHORT RUN SUSTAINABILITY

As discussed in the previous section, the government might not achieve its long-run economic targets immediately. As a result, in order to keep its stock of debt stable as a fraction of GDP, the Government might need to run a higher primary surplus than the -0.3 percent of GDP indicated above. Table 1 indicates a number of alternative scenarios that adjust one variable at a time to show that variable's effect on the required primary surplus.

Table 1 shows quite clearly that if growth is considerably more sluggish than targeted (as in the 2 percent growth scenario), then the government has a choice: run a higher primary surplus (by 1.8 percentage points of GDP), or let debt grow at that rate. The significance of a higher real interest rate is also demonstrated rather sharply in Table 1. If agents lose faith that a tight money

---

[102] The appendix derives this result.

policy is feasible in the long-run, and the Government starts paying a large premium on its nominal debt (as in the 11.5 percent real interest rate scenario) the effects on the Government's budget could be dramatic. A primary surplus of 3 percent of GDP might be needed to keep the level of debt stable.[103]

Finally, Table 1 also illustrates that allowing inflation to rise does little to help the government's fiscal position. Even with the inflation rate that maximizes seignorage (about 22 percent) the fiscal surplus that could be sustained would never be lower than -0.7 percent of GDP.

Table 1: Alternative Scenarios for the Short-Run Sustainable Primary Surplus

	Growth Rate of GDP (percent)	*Real interest rate (percent)*	*Inflation rate (percent)*	*Sustainable Primary Surplus (percent of GDP)*
Baseline	5	5.5	3.5	-0.3
Growth scenarios	2			1.5
	3	5.5	3.5	0.9
	4			0.3
Real interest rate scenarios		7.5		0.8
	5	9.5	3.5	1.9
		11.5		3.0
Inflation rate scenarios			6.5	-0.5
	5	5.5	9.5	-0.6
			12.5	-0.6

Source: Staff Calculations.

ALTERNATIVE ASSUMPTIONS ABOUT INITIAL DEBT

The baseline calculations done above used standard estimates of the Government's current level of indebtedness. These calculations might not be robust to taking into account: (i) potential future privatization revenue, (ii) estimates of contingent liabilities, (iii) and central bank reserves. To address this issue, consider Table 2, which computes the long-run sustainable fiscal surplus corresponding to different initial levels of debt.

Table 2: Initial Debt and the Long Run Sustainable Primary Surplus (percent of GDP)

Initial Debt	0	15	30	45	60	75
Primary Surplus	-0.6	-0.5	-0.5	-0.4	-0.3	-0.2

Source: Staff Calculations.

Table 2 is computed using the same parameters as in the baseline example earlier, in which the estimate of initial debt was taken to be 54.5 percent of GDP. With that level of initial debt, the sustainable primary surplus was, in fact, a deficit of 0.3 percent of GDP. Notice that this

---

[103] This calculation illustrates a generic fact about sustainability calculations. The initial debt stock and its associated servicing cost have little impact on the calculated sustainable surplus when the real interest rate is close to the real growth rate of the economy. Once the real interest rate exceeds the real growth rate, debt can accumulate very rapidly, and the size of the debt stock becomes important.

estimate is very robust to changes in the level of initial debt. Even with an assumption of zero initial debt, the sustainable primary deficit only rises to a mere 0.6 percent of GDP.

Why is the sustainable primary deficit so insensitive to assumptions about initial debt? This outcome results from another assumption of the baseline example—that the long-run real interest rate is only 50 basis points higher than the real growth rate of the economy. This means that every extra 10 percent of GDP in government debt adds only 0.05 percent of GDP in debt service costs in the long-run.

The correct interpretation of this finding is that the initial debt level is not particularly important in measuring the sustainable fiscal surplus for Croatia. What is more important is the sharp limit placed on seignorage by the estimated money demand curve—even in the absence of initial debt, the sustainable primary fiscal deficit is never greater than 0.6 percent of GDP.

If, regardless of this finding, one was to adjust the earlier estimate of initial debt (54.5 percent of GDP), one would need to subtract from it a measure of the central bank's reserve assets. At the end of 1999 these were on the order of HRK 23.1 billion, or about 16 percent of GDP. One would also need to subtract some estimate of the present value of likely future privatization revenues, which are estimated to be HRK 21.5 billion or about 15 percent of GDP. Finally, one would need to add in a rough estimate of contingent liabilities. These are notoriously difficult to estimate, but one estimate, by Standard and Poor's, that only includes liabilities that might be generated by the financial system, is on the order of 10–16 percent of GDP. This estimate is based on the size of the financial system relative to the economy, and on the likelihood of the Government being called upon to honor its explicit *and/or* implicit guarantees to the creditors of the system. Separately, the Government does its own accounting of financial and performance guarantees that it has explicitly taken on. At the end of 1999, the outstanding stock of such guarantees was about HRK 21.4 billion, or about 15 percent of GDP. However, this number does not translate directly into debt—to account for it as a debt some rule for making loss provisions would need to be applied.

Taken together, these various factors suggest an initial net debt level that could be as low as about 23 percent of GDP. However, this would only raise the sustainable deficit to 0.5 percent of GDP. More realistically, given the possibility that some government guaranteed loans will not be repaid without government assistance, the appropriate estimate of initial debt could be higher by several percent of GDP.

Again, this underlines the relative robustness of the results in this chapter. Because the debt service cost per unit of debt is being assumed to be very small in the long-run, the calculations are very conservative—more likely than not they *understate* the size of the primary surplus needed to achieve long run sustainability.

Has Recent Fiscal Policy Been Sustainable?

No—fiscal policy has moved quite sharply in the wrong direction in recent years, and it has done this even taking into account the effects of the 1998-99 downturn on the budget. This is confirmed by Table 3, which summarizes CCG budget operations in the period 1997–2000.

In 1997 the cyclically-adjusted primary deficit was about 2.2 percent of GDP, a figure that is quite far from the long-run level that is sustainable for Croatia, and well short of the short-run surpluses needed during times of slow growth or high real interest rates. But, starting in 1998, the Government ran adjusted primary deficits of 1.4 and 6.4 percent of GDP in 1998 and 1999, and continued to be substantially in deficit in 2000.

Table 3: Consolidated General Government Budgets 1997–2000 (percent of GDP)

	1997	1998	1999	2000*
Estimated Accrual Surplus	-2.9	-1.2	-3.6	-3.8
– *Privatization Revenue*	0.6	1.7	4.5	2.0
+ *Interest*	1.5	1.5	1.6	1.8
Implied Primary Surplus	-2.1	1.4	-6.5	-4.0
+ *Cyclical Adjustment*	-0.1	0.0	0.1	N/A
Adjusted Primary Surplus	-2.2	-1.4	-6.4	N/A

Source: Staff Calculations.

Apart from the basic considerations that are derived from Table 3 and the sustainable surplus calculations above, there is strong a priori evidence that fiscal policy is moving in the wrong direction. This evidence includes:

- The increased and heavy reliance of the Government on privatization revenue to close the budget.

- The apparent lack of potential new sources of government revenue—tax revenue already represents over 40 percent of GDP, and is a significant burden on the economy.

- Spiraling public sector wage costs. With the Government facing limits on its ability to raise revenue, its inability to rein in public sector wage increases has led it to cut other government spending on goods and services. Of course, cutting current spending items, such as operations and maintenance of public infrastructure, or cutting capital spending, can be a veil that hides a lack of longer run sustainability. Necessary expenditures can only be postponed so long.

- Burgeoning arrears.

- The fact that, even under optimistic scenarios, the Government faces a pension system financing gap of several percent of GDP for the coming decade.

In view of the above highlighted factors, it is difficult to be optimistic about the Government's ability to fix its financial situation without a major fiscal reform effort. To this end, the next subsection presents the elements of a credible fiscal consolidation in the context of Croatia.

ANNEX B: CONSTRUCTION OF THE CYCLICALLY ADJUSTED BALANCE

The primary balance (S) is expressed as the difference between revenues (R) and the primary expenditures (X):

$$S_t = R_t - X_t$$

The above expression in terms of GDP can be written as:

$$s_t = r_t - x_t$$

Following Chand, S_t is assumed to have two components: the discretionary component (S^D) and the non-discretionary component (S^N) that moves with the business cycle:

$$S_t = S_t^D + S_t^N$$

It is assumed that revenues move in proportion to GDP, Y_t, absent any changes in tax rates. Non-discretionary revenues can, then, be expressed as: $R_t^N = \hat{r}Y_t$. Holding tax rates unchanged, the above expression can be written as $r_t^N = \hat{r}$ so that discretionary revenue, as a fraction of GDP is $r_t^D = r_t - \hat{r}$.

Expenditures are assumed to be sensitive with respect to the trend in output—i.e., potential output. Therefore, any movement away from a path where expenditures are proportional to potential out is deemed discretionary. Put differently, it is assumed that $X_t^N = \hat{x}Y_t^*$ so that $x_t^N = \hat{x}Y_t^* / Y_t$ and $x_t^D = x_t - \hat{x}Y_t^* / Y_t$.

This suggests that s^D can be written as:

$$s_t^D = r_t^D - x_t^D = r_t - \hat{r} - (x_t - \hat{x}Y_t^* / Y_t) = r_t - x_t - (\hat{r} - \hat{x}Y_t^* / Y_t) = s_t - s_t^N$$

Hence, a practical way to calculate the cyclically adjusted budget would be to subtract an estimate of $\hat{r} - \hat{x}Y_t^* / Y_t$ from the actual primary balance. In the calculation of this term, two assumptions are made: (i) it is assumed that $\hat{r}$ is equal to the sample average of R_t/Y_t; (ii) it is assumed that $\hat{x}$ is equal to the sample average of X_t / Y_t^*.

ANNEX C: BUDGET MANAGEMENT

	Recommendation	Legislation / Administra-tive[a]	Priority[b]
I.1	Amend the Budget Law to include all EBFs in the Budget.	L	(1)
I.2	For the Children's Allowance Fund and Croatian Public Water Management Fund, consider making them programs within Ministries rather than separate funds.	L	(3)
I.3	All sources of public revenue should be brought on-budget.	L	(1)
I.4	Adopt modified accrual budgeting and accounting. This is the most assured method for resolving over-commitment of funds, as well as structural imbalances leading to over-spending in the public finance system.	L	(1)
I.5	Establish immediate commitment control by establishing a policy of MoF review and approval of all contracts prior to contract signature.	A	(1)
I.6	Within the budgetary accounting system, identify those programs or activities in which actual spending is driven by laws outside the budget cycle. This information will allow Government and Parliament to better understand the implications and limitations of annual budget decisions	A	(3)
I.7	Initiate a project within the budget office or MoF to identify all mandatory transfer of funds within the budget, such as the 2 percent transfer from capital projects to veterans programs. Unless there is a compelling rationale or public policy benefit, convert the programs funded through these transfers away from mandatory transfers to direct budget support.	A	(3)
II.1	To help benchmark forecasts used in the Budget and provide a better basis for judging if the forecast is too optimistic, collect economic forecasts from several leading private and public sector agencies. A table should be prepared comparing these independent forecasts, and explaining variations from the median of the sample of forecasts.	A	(1)
II.2	The Budget Law should be amended to require more transparency on the economic estimates underlying the budget.	L	(1)
II.3	Improve sectoral analysis underlying the budget. In the short-run, while other, more control-oriented budget process reforms are underway, the current analytical gap could perhaps be filled with targeted use of international assistance (World Bank, etc.).	A	(1)
II.4	Improve the use of analysis in the budget process. • developing the analytical capacity of the budget office staff (training), • expanding the number of young professional staff with analytical skills, • reorganizing the budget office to assign specific Ministries or sectors to budget office staff so that they develop program	A	(1)

		Recommendation	Legislation / Administrative[a]	Priority[b]
		and policy expertise in these areas. • Senior MoF staff should request analytical materials and options, including written policy papers, as part of the budget development process.		
II.5		Formally establish the budget office in the Budget Law, and designate its responsibilities, in order to highlight the importance of analysis and the work of the budget office. This includes assigning the budget office formal responsibility for preparing analytical materials in support of Government budget process.	L	(1)
II.6		Improve identification of programs in budget. The budget for each Ministry should be divided into major agencies (organizations within the Ministry), and each agencies subdivided into major programs and activities (ideally, in alignment with Ministry core activities—those statutory responsibilities assigned to the Ministry). And for each agency, the budget (at least as submitted to Parliament), should contain a brief paragraph (1 or 2 sentences) describing what the program does.	A L? Will require discussion with Parliament on new budget format.	(3)
II.7		The current chart of accounts should be overhauled to eliminate excess details, and focus reporting on key expenditure categories. The display of budget information in the Budget document should be revised, in conjunction with adoption of program budgeting, to illustrate what is being purchased by program funds.	A. L? Will require discussion with Parliament on new budget format.	(2)
II.8		Basic output measures should be incorporated into the annual budgets, reinforcing the budget process as the tool of government management and policy setting, aiding transparency and accountability, and beginning to link resources with results.	A	(2)
II.9		Task the head of the Budget Formulation Office with planning and implementing a more robust budget formulation process. To successfully implement this recommendation, it will likely be necessary to expand the number of staff in the Budget Formulation Office, as suggested in Recommendation 2.4, above.	A	(2)
II.10		Establish a Budget Officer's Council consisting of the senior budget official of each Ministry and chaired by the head of the MoF Budget Formulation Office. This council should hold regular meetings, and serve as a forum for discussing and planning improvements in the budget process.	A	(3)
II.11		Line Ministries should begin budget formulation prior to receipt of the MoF call letter. *By waiting until the call memorandum is received, Ministries have become passive participants in the budget process. At the very least, Ministries should have developed policies for various budget contingencies, identified*	A	(1)

	Recommendation	Legislation / Administra- tive[a]	Priority[b]
	options for reducing spending, and prepared sound proposals for any new initiatives or programs prior to receiving the call letter. Prepared in advance, the Ministry is in a far better position to react rationally to budget guidance from the MoF, and argue rationally for alternate resource allocations.		
II.12	Through training courses, the MoF and line Ministries actively seek to develop the budget and policy analysis capacity of line Ministry budget and finance offices.	A	(2)
II.13	Building on recommendations under 1.6 and 1.7, the MoF or Cabinet should expressly develop a policy regarding budgets for mandatory programs. Most important in this regard is a prohibition against budgeting less than full cost for mandatory programs unless specific legislation that will alter the program to meet available resources is drafted and transmitted with the annual budget (either as a separate legislation accompanying the budget, or as part of the budget law itself).	A	(1)
II.14	In the context of strengthening the budget process, an explicit multi-year framework should be developed to improve financial decision-making.	A	(1)
III.1	Negotiate with Parliament a new system of expenditure control that focuses on larger aggregations of funds. The level to which funds will be controlled should be stated in a new budget law.	A. L?	(2)
III.2	Until internal auditing and control are institutionalized in government, budget supervision audits should be conducted through to the end user or recipient of funds whenever possible.	A	(3)
III.3	Formally establish the BSO within the MoF through the budget law. The Office should be somewhat independent to pursue its mission, and report to the Minister or Deputy Minister of Finance.	L	(2)
III.4	Strengthen the BSO with additional staff and resources to properly carry-out its' duties.	A	(1)
III.5	The BSO should focus on ex post audits, with particular attention to evaluating the internal control and audit functions within each Ministry until such time as these functions are well established and operating effectively.	A	(1)
III.6	The BSO should also develop and issue guidance and standards for Ministry internal control and audit functions to assure quality and consistency. The BSO could also assist in developing professional standards of training for Ministry auditors.	A	(1)
III.7	Amend the budget law to strengthen the penalties for over-spending budgeted resources and violating the budget law, and clarify in the law what agency is responsible for monitoring compliance with the law and assigning penalties.	L	(1)
III.8	Ministries should transfer staff and resources from other activities as necessary to establish functioning internal control offices.	A	(1)

		Recommendation	Legislation / Administrative[a]	Priority[b]
III.9		The MoF should evaluate the applicability of the Ministry of Labor payment model for other line Ministries. If applicable, the Ministry of Labor should be highlighted as an example of good practice, and used as a center of excellence to support similar work in other Ministries. Identifying domestic centers of excellence and successful approaches to problems, disseminating the information, and capitalizing on the local expertise is an important component of building an organic, sustainable public expenditure management system.	A	(1)
III.10		As a medium or longer-term goal for development of the Croatian public expenditure system, the task of commissioning deeper program evaluations should be established and institutionalized. • Internal and external audits should be extended to include management and performance assessments. • In the near term, use external assistance and Public Expenditure Reviews to fill the analytical gap.	A	(3)
IV.1		The Sabor Chamber of Deputies BC should be supported with several professional staff dedicated to public expenditure analysis.	A	(2)
IV.2		The Government should improve budget communications to the Sabor through improvement in the quality and content of the annual budget submission to the Sabor.	A	(1)
IV.3		To support Sabor capacity for involvement in the budget process, the Government could: (a) prepare a Citizen's Guide to the Budget for Parliament; (b) offer brief (1-2 day) training to MP's on the budget, budget process, basic statutes, etc.	A	(2)
IV.4		The SAO should continue to focus on compliance and financial audits in the short term. Management and performance audits should be a longer-term goal of the SAO, after the current Croatian public expenditure system has further developed and stabilized.	A	(1)

a. The proposal can be implemented through administrative means (A) or required legislation (L).
b. Indicates the priority of the recommendations: Priority 1: implement as soon as possible; Priority 2: important, bur can be delayed; Priority 3: longer-term objectives

ANNEX D: STATISTICAL ANNEX

Table 1: Croatia: CGG Finances by Government Level, 1994-2000 (Cash Basis)

	As a percentage of GDP						
	1994	1995	1996	1997	1998	1999	2000
Total revenue and grants	45.6	47.6	49.7	48.3	51.5	48.2	45.9
Budgetary Central Gov.	26.1	27.8	28.5	27.2	30.8	28.2	26.5
Extrabudgetary funds	15.6	15.3	15.5	15.4	15.0	14.6	13.8
o.w. Pension Fund	8.1	8.6	8.7	8.6	7.4	7.4	7.0
o.w. Health Insurance Fund	4.3	4.6	4.8	4.7	5.9	6.0	5.6
Local government	3.9	4.4	5.7	5.7	5.7	5.4	5.5
Total expenditure and net lending	44.1	48.9	50.7	49.8	52.4	54.8	53.2
Budgetary Central Gov.	23.6	26.5	25.4	23.5	24.4	24.9	23.4
Extrabudgetary funds	16.9	18.3	19.7	20.6	22.1	24.1	23.9
o.w. Pension Fund	7.6	9.0	9.7	11.1	11.8	13.3	12.8
o.w. Health Insurance Fund	6.0	7.2	7.7	7.1	7.9	8.4	8.8
Local government	3.7	4.2	5.7	5.7	5.8	5.8	5.9
Overall cash deficit/surplus*	1.5	-1.4	-1.0	-1.5	-0.9	-6.5	-7.3
Budgetary Central Gov.	2.5	1.4	3.2	3.7	6.4	3.3	3.2
Extrabudgetary funds	-1.2	-3.0	-4.2	-5.2	-7.1	-9.5	-10.1
o.w. Pension Fund	0.5	-0.4	-1.0	-2.5	-4.4	-5.9	-5.8
o.w. Health Insurance Fund	-1.7	-2.6	-3.0	-2.4	-2.0	-2.3	-3.2
Local government	0.2	0.2	0.0	0.0	-0.1	-0.4	-0.4

*Privatization receipts as financing item.
Source: Ministry of Finance and Staff Calculations.

Table 2: Croatia: CGG Finances by Government Level, 1994-2000 (Accrual Basis)

	As a percentage of GDP						
	1994	1995	1996	1997	1998	1999	2000
Total revenue and grants	45.6	47.6	49.7	48.3	51.5	48.2	45.9
Budgetary Central Gov.	26.1	27.8	28.5	27.2	30.8	28.2	26.5
Extrabudgetary funds	15.6	15.3	15.5	15.4	15.0	14.6	13.8
o.w. Pension Fund	8.1	8.6	8.7	8.6	7.4	7.4	7.0
o.w. Health Insurance Fund	4.3	4.6	4.8	4.7	5.9	6.0	5.6
Local government	3.9	4.4	5.7	5.7	5.7	5.4	5.5
Total expenditure and net lending	44.1	48.9	51.9	51.3	53.9	56.2	51.3
Budgetary Central Gov.	23.6	26.5	25.6	24.1	25.1	25.7	23.1
Extrabudgetary funds	16.9	18.3	20.6	21.6	23.0	24.8	22.3
o.w. Pension Fund	7.6	9.0	9.7	11.1	11.8	13.9	12.3
o.w. Health Insurance Fund	6.0	7.2	8.6	8.0	8.8	8.5	7.7
Local government	3.7	4.2	5.7	5.7	5.8	5.8	5.9
Overall accrual deficit/surplus*	1.5	-1.4	-2.2	-3.0	-2.4	-8.0	-5.4
Budgetary Central Gov.	2.5	1.4	2.9	3.1	5.7	2.6	3.4
Extrabudgetary funds	-1.2	-3.0	-5.1	-6.1	-8.0	-10.2	-8.5
o.w. Pension Fund	0.5	-0.4	-1.0	-2.5	-4.4	-6.5	-5.3
o.w. Health Insurance Fund	-1.7	-2.6	-3.9	-3.3	-2.9	-2.5	-2.1
Local government	0.2	0.2	0.0	0.0	-0.1	-0.4	-0.4

*Privatization receipts as financing item.
Source: Ministry of Finance and Staff Calculations.

Table 3: Croatia - Consolidated General Government, Economic Classification, Cash Basis

(as % of GDP)	1994	1995	Outturn 1996	1997	1998	Estimate 1999	2000
I. Total revenue and grants	46.0	48.2	50.4	48.6	52.9	52.6	47.7
III. Current revenue	45.6	47.2	48.9	47.6	50.8	47.7	45.2
IV. Tax revenue	43.2	44.4	44.4	43.0	46.9	43.7	41.4
1. Taxes on individual income	6.1	5.8	6.4	5.4	5.9	5.3	4.6
2. Taxes on corporate income	1.0	1.4	1.6	2.0	2.5	2.3	1.8
3. Social security contributions	13.2	14.1	14.4	14.3	14.0	13.6	12.9
4. Taxes on property	0.3	0.5	0.5	0.6	0.6	0.5	0.5
5. General sales tax / VAT	15.0	13.0	12.5	12.2	16.1	14.2	14.0
6. Excises	3.1	5.0	5.0	4.3	4.2	4.3	4.9
7. Local taxes on goods and services	0.4	0.1	0.1	0.1	0.1	0.1	0.1
8. Taxes on international trade and transactions	4.0	4.0	3.7	3.8	3.1	3.0	2.4
9. Other tax revenues	0.3	0.4	0.2	0.2	0.4	0.3	0.3
V. Nontax revenues	2.4	2.8	4.5	4.6	4.0	3.9	3.8
VI. Capital revenue	0.4	1.0	1.5	1.0	2.0	4.9	2.5
VII. Grants	0.0	0.0	0.0	0.0	0.0	0.0	0.0
I. Total expenditures and lending Minus repayments	44.1	48.9	50.7	49.8	52.4	54.8	53.2
III. Current expenditures	40.7	44.1	43.5	43.3	44.6	46.5	46.6
1. Expenditures for goods and services	25.9	27.8	25.2	23.2	24.7	24.1	24.6
1.1. Wages and salaries	10.4	11.9	11.2	11.0	11.9	12.7	12.4
1.3. Other purchases of goods and services	15.6	15.9	14.0	12.2	12.8	11.4	12.1
2. Interest payments	1.3	1.4	1.2	1.5	1.5	1.7	1.8
3. Subsidies and current transfers	13.5	14.9	17.2	18.7	18.4	20.8	20.2
3.1. Subsidies	2.4	2.1	2.2	2.1	2.7	2.7	2.8
3.3. Transfers to nonprofit institutions	1.6	1.5	2.2	2.2	1.1	1.1	1.1
3.4. Transfers to households	9.5	11.2	12.7	14.3	14.5	16.4	16.0
3.5. Transfers abroad	0.1	0.1	0.1	0.1	0.1	0.5	0.3
IV. Capital expenditures	3.1	4.5	6.8	6.0	6.9	7.2	5.8
4. Acquisition of fixed capital assets	2.5	2.5	3.5	3.1	4.0	4.7	3.3
5. Purchases of stocks	0.2	0.0	0.0	0.0	0.0	0.0	0.0
6. Purchases of land and intangible assets	0.0	0.0	0.3	0.3	0.3	0.3	0.4
7. Capital transfers	0.3	2.0	3.0	2.6	2.6	2.1	2.0
	0.0	0.0	0.0	0.0	0.0	0.0	0.0
V. Lending minus repayments	0.4	0.3	0.5	0.5	0.9	1.1	0.8
Current deficit/surplus	4.8	3.1	5.4	4.3	6.2	1.1	-1.4
Total deficit/surplus	1.8	-0.7	-0.4	-1.2	0.5	-2.2	-5.5

Source: Ministry of Finance and Staff Calculations.

Table 4: Croatia - Consolidated General Government, Economic Classification, Accrual Basis

Accrual basis	1994	1995	1996	1997	1998	1999	2000
Total revenue and grants	45.6	47.5	49.7	48.3	51.5	48.2	45.9
Tax revenue	43.2	44.4	44.4	43.0	46.9	43.7	41.4
Nontax revenue	2.4	2.8	4.5	4.6	4.0	4.0	3.9
Capital revenue	0.04	0.3	0.8	0.7	0.6	0.6	0.6
Grants	0.0	0.0	0.0	0.0	0.04	0.0	0.0
Total expenditure and net lending	44.1	48.9	51.9	51.3	53.9	56.2	51.3
Current expenditure	40.7	44.1	44.3	44.3	45.6	47.5	45.3
Wages and salaries	10.4	11.9	11.2	11.0	11.9	12.7	12.4
Other purchases of goods and services	15.6	15.9	14.6	12.9	13.6	12.2	11.2
Interest payments	1.3	1.5	1.2	1.5	1.5	1.7	1.8
Subsidies	2.4	2.1	2.2	2.2	2.7	2.8	2.7
Current transfers	11.1	12.8	15.2	16.8	15.9	18.3	17.1
Capital expenditure	3.1	4.6	7.2	6.5	7.4	7.6	5.2
Net lending	0.4	0.3	0.5	0.5	0.9	1.1	0.8
Current surplus	4.8	3.1	4.6	3.3	5.2	0.1	-0.1
Deficit/surplus*	1.5	-1.4	-2.2	-3.0	-2.5	-8.0	-5.4
*privatization receipts below the line	0.4	0.7	0.6	0.3	1.4	4.3	1.9

Source:

REFERENCES

Adam Smith Institute. 1997. "Reform of Public Administration in the Republic of Croatia." Mimeo, September.

Akrap, Andelko, and Jakov Gelo. 1999. "Demographic Research in Croatia, First Phase of the Project: Estimate of Population in Croatia in 1998 according to Sex and Age Structure." University of Zagreb, Faculty of Economics.

Alesina, Alberto, and Roberto Perotti. 1995. "Fiscal Expansions and Adjustments in OECD Countries." *Economic Policy* 21 (October): 205–48.

Antos, Joseph. 1999. "Croatia: Health Financing Issues and Options." Report prepared for the World Bank.

Barbone, L., and R. Polastri. 1998. "Hungary's Public Finances in an International Context, in Public Finance Reform during the Transition." The World Bank, Washington D.C.

Berman, Peter. 1998. "Rethinking Health Care Systems: Private Health Care Provision in India." *World Development* 26(8): 1463–79.

Berman, Peter, and Mukesh Chawla. 2000. "A Model for Analyzing Strategic Use of Government Financing to Improve Health Care Provision." Harvard School of Public Health, Partnerships for Health Reform Project, Major Applied Research 4, Technical Paper 1, Boston, Massachusetts.

Berryman, Sue E., with Ivan Drabek, Marcelo Bisogno, Joe E. Colombano and Sanja Madžarević-Šujster. 2000. "The Croatia Education System." Mimeo, December.

Bidani, B., and M. Ravallion. 1997. "Decomposing social indicators using distributional data." *Journal of Econometrics*, 77, 125–139.

Bisogno, Marcelo. 2000. "The Croatian Labor Market in Transition." Technical Background Paper to Croatia Economic Vulnerability and Welfare Study. World Bank, Washington, DC.

Bisogno, M. and S.Madžarević-Šujster. 2000. "Croatia: Fiscal Performance Review and Prospects 1991-2000." Policy Note, mimeo, January.

Brander et. al. 1998. "Structural Budget Deficits and Sustainability of Fiscal Positions in the European Union." Oesterreichische National Bank Working Paper, No. 26.

Buiter, Willem H. 1989. "Some Thoughts on the Role of Fiscal Policy in Stabilization and Structural Adjustment in Developing Countries," in Willem H. Buiter, ed., Principles of Budgetary and Financial Policy. Cambridge, Massachusetts: MIT Press.

Burnside, Craig and Ilker Domac. 2000. "Croatia: Achieving Fiscal Sustainability." Mimeo, December.

Castel, Paulette. 2000a. "The Pension sector in Croatia." Mimeo, December. With contributions from David Lindeman, Philip O'Keefe and Zoran Anusic.

--- 2000b. "Poverty Among Elderly. Simulating the Impact of Pension Reform." World Bank, July.

Chawla, Mukesh. 2000. "The Health sector in Croatia." Mimeo, December. With contributions from S. Madžarević-Šujster and Ivan Drabek.

Cochrane, John. 2000. "Long-term Debt and Optimal Policy in the Fiscal Theory of the Price Level", forthcoming in Econometrica.

Croatian Health Insurance Institute. 1999a. "Decision on the Basis for Concluding Contracts with Health-Care Institutions and Private Health-Care Providers", third session of the Executive Council of the Croatian Health Insurance Institute, 15 May 1999.

Croatian Health Insurance Institute. 1999b. "Regulations on the Standards and Norms Governing Compulsory Health Insurance Entitlements", third session of the Executive Council of the Croatian Health Insurance Institute, 15 May 1999.

Croatia Official Gazette, different years.

Defever, Mia. 1995. "Health Care Reforms: The Unfinished Agenda", *Health Policy* 34 (1995): 1-7.

Dorotinsky, William. 2000. "Budgetary Management Assessment – Republic of Croatia." Mimeo, June. Prepared for USAID.

Easterly, William R. 1999. "When is Fiscal Adjustment an Illusion." *Economic Policy*, 28 April, pp 57-86.

Easterly, W. and S. Fischer. 1990. "The Economics of the Government Budget Constraint", The World Bank Research Observer, Vol.5, No.2, July.

European Observatory of Health Care Systems. 1999. "Health Care Systems in Transition: Croatia", WHO Regional Office for Europe.

Gatti, Roberta. 2000. "The Economics of Decentralization: a Review of the Literature and the Case of Education Provision." World Bank, Washington, DC.

Girishankar, Navin. 1999. "Reforming Institutions for Service Delivery: A Framework for Development Assistance with an Application to the Health, Nutrition, and Population Portfolio." *Policy Research Working Paper 2039*. World Bank, Washington, DC.

Hammer, Jeffrey S. 1997. "Health and Education Expenditures in Karnataka." *Policy Research Department*, World Bank, Washington, DC.

Hsiao, William C. 1995. "Abnormal Economics in the Health Sector." *Health Policy* 32 (1995): 125-139.

IMF, Fiscal Affairs Department. 2000. "Croatia a Review of Tax Policy." Mimeo, June.

IMF, Government Finance Statistics, 1991-1997

IMF, Republic of Croatia. 1999. "Selected Issues and Statistical Appendix." December 22.

Jimenez, E. 1987. "Pricing Policy in the Social Sectors. Cost Recovery for Education and Health in Developing Countries." World Bank, The Johns Hopkins University Press.

Kuzman, Marina. 2000. "Operations of Inpatients Institutions in Croatia in 1999." Draft.

Ladavac, Jelena. 2000. "Public Expenditure Review: Fiscal Decentralization." In draft. World Bank, Washington, DC.

Madzarevic-Sujster S. 2000. "Croatia: Social Expenditure 1994-1999." Mimeo, World Bank.

Mahal, Ajay. 2000. "Public expenditures on health in India." Draft Manuscript prepared for The World Bank.

Mechanic, David. 1999. "Issues in Promoting Health." Social Science and Medicine, Vol. 48, No. 6.

Musgrove, P. 1996. "Public and Private Roles in Health. Theory and Financing Patterns." *World Bank Discussion Paper* No. 339. Washington, DC.

Nandakumar, A.K., Mukesh, Chawla and Miriam Khan. 2000. "Utilization of Outpatient Care in Egypt and its Implications for the Role of Government in Health Care Provision." World Development, vol. 28, no. 1, January, 2000.

OECD (Organization for Economic Cooperation and Development). Various years. Education at a Glance: OECD Indicators. Paris: Center for Educational Research and Innovation, OECD.

Parker, Peter. 2000. "The Transport sector in Croatia." Mimeo, December 2000.

Paul, Samuel. 1991. "Accountability in Public Services: Exit, Voice, and Capture." *Working Paper Series 614*. World Bank, Washington, DC.

Republic of Croatia - Ministry of Finance, Annual Report of the Ministry of Finance, 1997, 1998 & 1999.

Republic of Croatia - Ministry of Finance, Monthly Statistical Review, various volumes, 1997—2000.

Republic of Croatia, Ministry of Health. 2000. "Health System Reform: The Strategy and Plan for the Reform of the Health Care System and Health Insurance of the Republic of Croatia." June.

Republic of Croatia. 2000. "The Basis for the Education system in the Republic of Croatia: Proposal for Discussion." Zagreb: Ministry of Education and Sport and Council of Education, June.

Sargent, Thomas and Neil Wallace. 1981. "Some Unpleasant Monetarist Arithmetic." Federal Reserve Bank of Minneapolis Quarterly Review 5 (Fall): 1—17.

Škreb, M. 1998. "Economic Transition in Croatia: An Insider's View," SAIS Review, vol. 18:71-88, Summer-Fall.

Sims, Christopher. 1994. "A Simple Model for the Determination of the Price Level and the Interaction of Monetary and Fiscal Policy." *Economic Theory*, 4, pp. 381–99.Urban Institute, Local Government Reform Project – Croatia, Review of the Legal framework, Mimeo, February 2001.

United States Agency for International Development (USAID. 2000. "Croatia Fiscal Assessment Report." Mimeo, February.

Woodford, Michael. 1995. "Price Level Determinacy Without Control of a Monetary Aggregate." Carnegie-Rochester Conference Series on Public Policy, 43 (December): 1—46.

World Bank. 1993. *World Development Report 1993*: "Investing in Health." Oxford University Press, New York.

World Bank. 1997. "An International Statistical Survey of Government Employment." Mimeo.

World Bank. 1997. "Croatia: Country Economic Memorandum. Croatia Beyond Stabilization." Report No. 17261-HR. December.

World Bank. 1999. "Croatia: Health Policy Note." Document Number: XXX HR, Draft of February 24.

World Bank. 2000a. "Croatia: A Policy Agenda for Reform and Growth." Mimeo, February 14.

World Bank. 2000b. "Hidden Challenges to Education Systems in Transition Economies." World Bank, Washington, DC.

World Bank. 2000c. *World Development Report 1999-2000*: "Entering the 21st century." Oxford University Press, New York.

World Bank. 2001. *Poverty Report*, "Croatia: Economic Vulnerability and Welfare Study." Report No 22079-HR, April.

World Health Organization. 2000. *The World Health Report 2000*, Geneva.

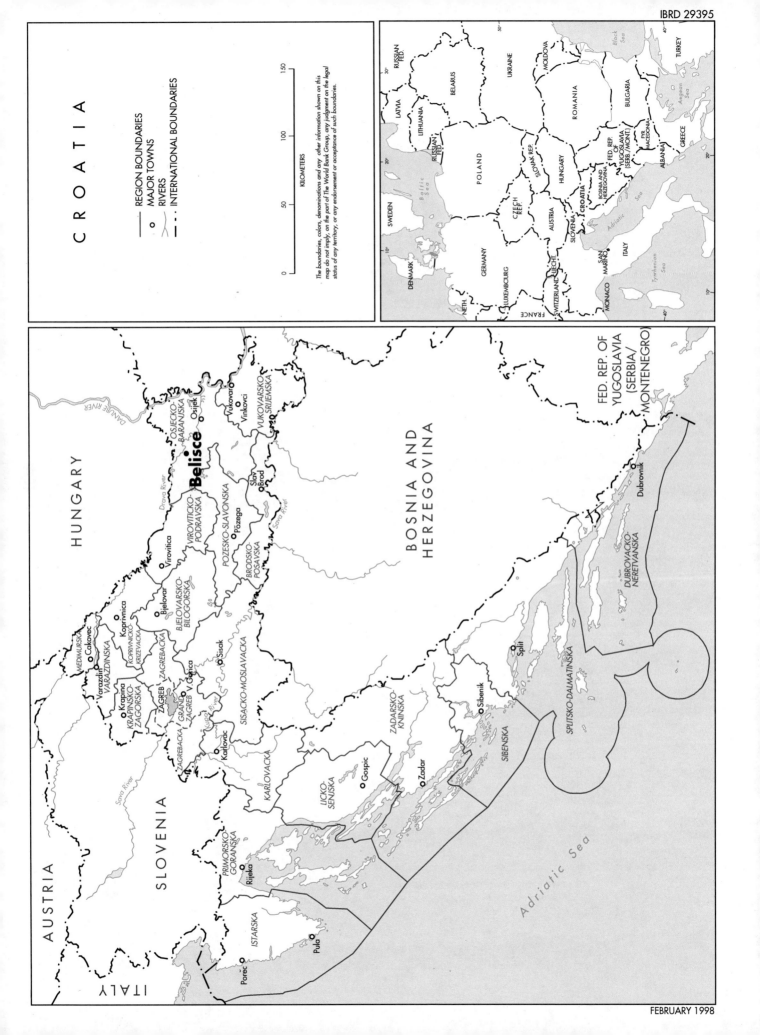

IBRD 29395

CROATIA

REGION BOUNDARIES
MAJOR TOWNS
RIVERS
INTERNATIONAL BOUNDARIES

KILOMETERS
0   50   100   150

The boundaries, colors, denominations and any other information shown on this map do not imply, on the part of The World Bank Group, any judgment on the legal status of any territory, or any endorsement or acceptance of such boundaries.

AUSTRIA
HUNGARY
SLOVENIA
ITALY
BOSNIA AND HERZEGOVINA
FED. REP. OF YUGOSLAVIA (SERBIA/MONTENEGRO)

DANUBE RIVER
Drava River
Sava River
Kupa River

MEDIMURSKA
Cakovec
VARAZDINSKA
Varazdin
KRAPINSKO-ZAGORSKA
Krapina
ZAGREB
ZAGREBACKA
V. Gorica
GRAD ZAGREB
Karlovac
KARLOVACKA
PRIMORSKO-GORANSKA
Rijeka
ISTARSKA
Pula
Porec
KOPRIVNICKO-KRIZEVACKA
Koprivnica
BJELOVARSKO-BILOGORSKA
Bjelovar
Sisak
SISACKO-MOSLAVACKA
VIROVITICKO-PODRAVSKA
Virovitica
POZESKO-SLAVONSKA
Pozega
OSJECKO-BARANJSKA
Osijek
Belisce
BRODSKO-POSAVSKA
Slav Brod
VUKOVARSKO-SRIJEMSKA
Vukovar
Vinkovci
LICKO-SENJSKA
Gospic
ZADARSKO-KNINSKA
Zadar
SIBENSKA
Sibenik
SPLITSKO-DALMATINSKA
Split
DUBROVACKO-NERETVANSKA
Dubrovnik

Adriatic Sea

FEBRUARY 1998